A Silly Idea

A catalogue record of this book is available from the British Library

First Edition: December 2003

ISBN: 1-84375-071-6

To order additional copies of this book please visit:
http://www.upso.co.uk/gezclark

Published by: UPSO Ltd
5 Stirling Road, Castleham Business Park,
St Leonards-on-Sea, East Sussex TN38 9NW UK
Tel: 01424 853349 Fax: 0870 191 3991
Email: info@upso.co.uk Web: http://www.upso.co.uk

A Silly Idea

The Lunatics Lurch

by

Gez Clark

UPSO

Introduction

It All Started as a Silly Idea!

I had had this idea for years. A walk from Lands End to Lenham. Why? I have no idea! But over the years the thought just kept coming back, more than just a thought, a dream, that I think I always knew I would attempt at some point in my life. It would have to be for charity, it was too big an event to do for no productive end.

Then, talking to Harry Appleton in The Red Lion one evening, having learnt that the fundraising for the new Lenham Community Centre had almost come to a halt, I decided that now was the time.

I didn't ask for volunteers to accompany me, I just started mentioning to certain people what I had in mind . I say "certain people" because I was hoping that somebody would volunteer to walk with me, and I didn't want drunken, insane, or otherwise similarly afflicted people to come forward!

Barrie Thomas (also known as Mouse) was the first volunteer. Drunken, insane, AND otherwise similarly afflicted, he's an old mate and I couldn't turn him down! Then Neil Osborne. Much the same really, but I knew that he is an ex-army man, and he would know exactly what he was letting himself in for!

An initial meeting was planned to bounce around some ideas and agree a basic plan for the route, training schedule, sponsorship, accommodation etc. It was now October 2001 and we had to get moving to take advantage of everybody's generosity over the Christmas season. We decided that the best time of year to do the walk would be May, as the weather wouldn't be too hot, and there was a fair chance that the rain might hold off for most of the time. HA HA HA ! We agreed that training would start in February to give us three months to prepare our feet and legs. Starting training in February was a great idea as I had already booked two weeks holiday in Bali for the end of that month! We then turned our thoughts to accommodation, and Mouse suggested that I should join the Royal Antediluvian Order of Buffaloes (as both he and Neil were already members) and we should approach the various Lodges along the way to provide a roof over our heads and maybe a plate of something nourishing. This I eventually agreed to, and am glad I did, although not for the obvious reason!

It was also decided that to gain maximum sponsorship from our efforts we should adopt a national charity and split the proceeds straight down the middle. The charity chosen was National Childrens' Homes, or N.C.H. (Action For Kids), to share the proceeds with the New Lenham Community Centre. Then a suggestion was made that I should do some Town Crying en route, to add a bit of colour to the walk. I agreed to this feeling that not only would it add colour to the walk, it was also a good way of attracting media interest. Well it added colour, anyway!

Into November now, and I approached The Ordnance Survey and several outlets to obtain free or cheap maps with which to start planning our route. The O. S. do not deal with the general public, and suggested that I contact my local Scout and Guide shop. The best deal came from "Outdoors", the Scout and Guide shop at the bottom of Gabriels Hill, Maidstone, where I was offered a 25% discount, and I bought all the relevant maps, seventeen in all, using the Explorer series on a scale of 1:25000 (two and a half inches to the mile!). I also invested in a "map wheel", a marvellous little tool for measuring distances on maps and converting them to miles. Only when we studied the maps and measured our first day's distance did we come to realise exactly what a task we had undertaken. The route planning alone was exhausting! Trying to get all three of us together to agree a route was proving impossible, so I started to put it together on my own. We all wanted to do as much of the walk as we could on footpaths as opposed to roads, so I thought "easy, draw a straight line from (a) to (b) on the map, then pick the footpaths that run closest to the line!" So I did that. Then I realised that the footpath that starts closest to the line usually takes a turn in the wrong direction and leads to a dead end in a field full of angry bullocks, (or so my imagination told me!). Suffice to say that the route planning took a lot longer than initially anticipated, especially when you are trying to avoid going directly across banks of contour lines.

Trying to draw a balance between the most direct route and the most scenic route is also a nightmare! The South-West Coastal Path looked tortuous, but was obviously going to provide some of the most spectacular scenery. Any vantage point will almost certainly be the highest point around, so there were, as in any walk of life (no pun intended), efforts to be made to gain the best views. This was relevant all the way back, not just in the west country, although the terrain in the west country made everything more difficult. We also had to decide the best routes around the various river estuaries, and combining all this with calculating every day's overnight stops was extremely time consuming. I still had not finished planning the route at Christmas!

In January I started writing letters to several national and local companies requesting sponsorship in the form of free or cheap footwear, waterproof clothing, publicity, and any other kind of practical support. Then came the depression. Negative responses from Walkers crisps, Adidas, Hi-Tec, Nike, Reebok, and Jessops cameras. But then I suppose at least they had the decency to reply. NONE, I repeat NONE of the local companies I wrote to in and around Lenham even bothered to reply to my letters. If this was a letter to a newspaper it would be signed "Disgusted, of Lenham!"

On a more positive note, the sponsorship forms around the village, especially in the Red Lion, had been doing very well. All the local shops and people who had offered to display the forms and posters were doing us proud! My love of the village may have been temporarily dented by the lack of support from the local companies, but the village community proved itself to be strong, and that is far more important than a bunch of company directors sitting round a table wringing their hands and counting their profits!

The Downs Mail and The Kent Messenger printed several articles each, some even with photographs! Then more doom and gloom. No response from any of the T.V. or radio stations. I had made several telephone calls to Meridian T.V., both Maidstone and Southampton, and to West Country T.V., and had written letters to them and Radio Kent, Invicta Radio, and Radio Five live. No interest at all. I just wonder how much more money we might have raised had we got more media coverage. Did these companies not realise just how much effort we were going to?!

Then all of a sudden it was February, and we were due to commence our training. We got off to a good start by walking from Neil's place in Langley back to Lenham one Sunday lunchtime, but that was only one walk, and we did that in our trainers! We hadn't got footwear organised, or waterproofs or anything! So Neil and I went to Maidstone to try to bully some poor shop owner or manager into giving us either free or heavily discounted goods. We tried a few of the footwear shops in the Chequers Centre and Week Street, before I remembered about my earlier success at "Outdoors". So off we went down Gabriels Hill to find that Outdoors was closed for lunch! But the shop next door, Baldocks Menswear was open, and they sell all the sort of gear we were looking for, so in we went. To say that the staff were helpful would be a dramatic understatement!! They were also very encouraging, and we agreed to purchase all our boots, waterproofs, and anything else we might need from there. They didn't offer us a specific rate of discount, but we reckon that we ended up with about £400 worth of gear for just over £170! We'll certainly be going back there for more when we need anything.

I had been promised free travel with Connex South-East from Headcorn to Waterloo, and had received an acknowledgement from First Great Western from my letter asking for transport from Waterloo to Truro, so at least the transport to Lands End was sorted. I had put some posters up around the village during March asking for volunteers to take some holiday and provide a support vehicle for us, and had had a great response from the village. We now had support organised all the way from Lands End to Lenham. BRILLIANT! Now all I had to do was organise accommodation for us. The Royal Antediluvian Order of Buffaloes (also known as "The Buffs") seemed to have let us down. Very disappointing considering their charitable status. We had one night organised through the Town Crier of Exmouth, Garth Gibson, one night through the Town Crier of Winchester, Alan Kinge, one night staying with friends of mine in Rusthall, near Tunbridge Wells, and two nights in Par, near Fowey, organised by the N.C.H. rep., Roger Francis.

Then I got a call from "Ben Forth", from Newton Abbot Buffs. We were welcome to stay with him, and he would feed and water us, and set us off with a good breakfast the following morning. Maybe this was the start of a mass response from the Buffs. But then again maybe not. We had no more correspondence from the Buffs at all!

March arrived to find us all so busy that we couldn't get together to practice our walking. This may sound silly, and a pretty feeble excuse, but we had to train together to adjust our pace so that we were all comfortable walking together. Neil had been doing a fair amount of training, Mouse a bit less, and I had been lazing about in the Indonesian sunshine! We then decided that we would train independently, and I set myself targets for each week until the start of the Lurch. These targets were pretty demanding when you think that I was working as well. Over the Easter weekend I walked sixty three miles. Fourteen on Good Friday, seventeen on Easter Saturday, eight (and a few trips up the Church tower) on Easter Sunday, and twenty four on the Monday. Most of these walks were over the roughest terrain I could find around Lenham, e.g. up on the North Downs. I was confident that I was prepared by then! Just about all ready then? The weekend before the Lurch Neil and I went and dragged Mouse out for a walk! Up to the Pilgrims' Way, up Flint Lane, left at the top to the top of Stede Hill, then right, right again past Hogbarn Caravan Park, down to White Post, right again towards Doddington and home via West Street and Lenham Hill. Mouse didn't seem too happy after that eight mile jaunt, and I was worried, but he assured us that he would be okay. So, we were all set!!!

Then, on the Monday before we were due to leave, I received a letter from First Great Western Trains to say that as they had already allocated all their charitable funding for the year, they would not be able to help with our transport from Waterloo to Truro! I made a very loud and not very polite 'phone call to their Public Relations Office without getting any further than their trains normally do, and went to see Jane at Headcorn station to see if she could suggest anything else, as it had been she who had helped me so far. She gave me a number for West Country Trains, and I gave them a call. I left my details with the young lady who answered my call, and didn't really expect to hear anything else about it, resigning myself to the fact that we would have to pay our fares from Waterloo onwards. On the Wednesday, as I was fighting my way through the traffic of west London, I got a call from the same young lady, who had obviously put a lot of effort into the matter, and she said she would post a concessionary ticket to me that day! She was as good as her word, and on the Thursday, the ticket arrived at my home, covering all three of us, from Waterloo to Truro on Saturday 11th May. The young lady shall remain nameless, as she requested no publicity, and I fear she may have jeopardised her position by arranging this ticket, but our gratitude is boundless for her efforts. And stuff the other company who wouldn't help!!!

The account you are about to read is how Neil and I recall the walk. After taking legal advice I decided to change some of the names to avoid causing embarrassment or incurring legal action! Mouse may have other memories which I haven't included, but each one of us can only recount what we individually recall, and I have tried to make this as complete an account as I possibly can, of all aspects of the walk.

Chapter 1

The First Five Days

Saturday 11th May. Nick Osborne (no relation to Neil) picked me up at 1015 in the morning, and we drove round and picked Mouse up from Maidstone Road and then on to get Neil at Langley. All our luggage just about filled the back of Nick's estate car! How the hell were we going to get all that off one train, across platforms and onto another? Never mind, if we have to perform a shuttle between trains then so be it! We offloaded ourselves and our luggage at Headcorn station, said our farewells to Nick, who bade us good luck, and struggled with all our gear over the bridge onto the London bound platform.

As we were waiting for the train, we were on the receiving end of some strange looks, and some out and out giggles from the youngsters! I suppose we must have looked a strange crew, three of us, all over six foot tall, dressed in walking boots, combat trousers, T shirts and an array of "different" headwear! Then some friends of mine, Ulrich and Paulette, from Biddenden turned up to catch the train for a day out in London, and as we told them where we were off to and why, their eyes opened wider and wider, and a promise of sponsorship came forth! (The epilogue details the particular sponsorship mentioned here.) Then, wonder of wonders, the train arrived bang on time, 1103, and we proceeded to clutter the guard's van with three rucksacks, with various bits attached, three smaller haversacks, a flight bag full of maps, compass, torch etc., three sleeping bags and all our waterproofs, water bottles, silly hats, Town Criers outfit and a cuddly toy! (Only joking).

We were all in pretty high spirits, and spent most of our one hour journey joking and chatting amongst ourselves, and looking out of the windows marvelling at the scenery which we've lived alongside most of our lives. The North Downs are so beautiful (especially when the sun shines!), it's a shame we take them so much for granted just because we see them every day. The people on the train seemed oblivious to the fact that they were sharing the journey with three heroic explorers, and we felt almost sorry for them, that they were just going to town for the day, and we had such an adventure in front of us! We arrived at Waterloo East at 1206 (still on time!) to discover that it's about 300 yards to Waterloo Main from where our next train departs. So we load ourselves up with all our bags and trudge wearily across to the main station. (Wearily? It's only midday for Heaven's sake!) Check which platform and what time to be there and grab a quick burger (it's like a beef burger only without the beef!) before making our way to platform 7 to catch the 1235 to Exeter St. Davids.

Trundling along watching the views, happily laughing away to ourselves, oblivious to the pain and suffering we were about to force upon our feet and legs, not to mention our wallets and stomachs, Neil pointed out some places he knew (usually through being involved with a woman!) as the train rattled along, Tisbury being one of them, and a smashing little fellow pushing a trolley appeared. Mouse deliberates for some time before ordering a cup of tea (or was it coffee? I can't remember, I was laughing so much!), Neil carefully selects a can of beer, as do I. Mouse hadn't looked as far as the lower shelf of the trolley! During the journey our tickets were checked, and we were informed that our complimentary ticket from South-West Trains would only get us as far as Exeter, as they only run to Truro on weekdays! Oh sh*t. Never mind, we won't tell anyone if you don't! We kept our spirits up pretty well all the way to Exeter, and once again unloaded our bags onto the platform. I went and checked which platform we needed for the next stage of our journey, and was delighted to discover that we only had to lug our bags about ten yards to the other side of the platform, so we had a quick smoke before the train arrived. It was only just after 4 o'clock when the train pulled into the station, so we were well ahead of time.

The train was actually the Edinburgh to Penzance holiday special, and was packed to the gunwales with Scots and North country folk, but we managed to find enough seats and luggage space to squeeze into, and settled down to what we thought was going to be the worst part of the journey.

Then my Town Criers bell fell out of its bag! Of course, all the other passengers wanted to know why I was carrying a handbell, so we had to tell them. After a mile or so of persuasion, I agreed to change into my outfit and try to raise a bit of sponsorship along the train. Now, if you have never tried to change your clothing on a crowded high speed train, let me tell you it's not easy! Standing at the end of the corridor with one foot halfway into the wrong leg of a pair of breeches while the train careers round a tight bend trying to eject every unsecured object through the window is not my idea of fun. Then why was I laughing so much? No matter, I rejoined Mouse and Neil in my red white and black 18th Century outfit and gave the rest of the carriage a twirl, then Neil and I set off along the train, Neil carrying the hat, me with my big mouth and bell, and started to raise some money. About two seconds into my first cry a voice next to me pleaded with me to stop, because I was waking the children. No problem, I can shout quietly! The reception we got all along the train was terrific, even when we arrived at the guards van. The guard, a lady guard, led us to the train manager's compartment, and the (lady) manager took us on to the buffet car, and instructed her staff to provide us with free tea, coffee, and sticky cakes! We weren't about to argue with that, and once we had blagged enough for all three of us we retraced our steps to rejoin Mouse. A quick count revealed we had collected £130! It was worth all the hassle of getting changed.

We arrived early into Truro and met Alan Jewell, the Town Crier of Redruth on the platform as arranged, at ten past six. He looked splendid in his bright blue outfit, and as I had never shouted next to, or opposite, or for that matter anywhere near another Town Crier, I began to wonder whether my voice would measure up! He greeted us with a welcoming cry, and I responded, thanking him for his time and decibels, and I think I did alright!! Unfortunately he had to leave immediately to attend a family birthday party, so we never had a chance to get to know each other properly, but I expect we'll meet at a competition somewhere, sometime. My sister and brother-in-law, Alison and Drew, met us at the station and I changed back into "civvies" before heading off to the pub.

The Old Ale House in Truro is a marvellous watering hole, with a fine selection of real ales, but after a couple of pints we needed something solid inside us, so we wandered off to look for a place to eat. After a reasonable pie and chips from the local chippie we decided to explore the back streets of Truro for some more pubs. We found one more, and once inside we got chatting to the locals, one of whom called his cousin and arranged our night's accommodation. We were a bit wary of accepting an unseen B & B, but we had little choice. I spoke to the landlord of the B & B on the phone, got directions, and arranged to be there by ten thirty, then we thanked our drinking companions, and made our way back to meet Alison and Drew at The Old Ale House. Drew drove me to the B & B to unload our bags, and I persuaded the owners to part with a key "just in case" we were late, then we went back to the pub for a couple more pints. As I said, The Old Ale House sells a wonderful selection of real ales, and we couldn't drag ourselves away until we had sampled at least four of them, could we?! The taxi got us back to the B & B at about eleven thirty, into the most beautiful rooms we could have wished for. The whole place looked as though it should have been a five-star hotel but on a much smaller scale. If you're ever in Truro looking for a night's accommodation, ask for The Mowhay. You won't be disappointed.

Tomorrow's the big day. I'm excited, but the beer soon sends me to sleep!

Sunday morning, the 12th of May. What a breakfast! We couldn't have asked for more. The house was magnificent, and built, we discovered, almost entirely by the proprietor, Mark, who is a stonemason, and a smashing bloke. The true beauty of the house was only revealed, however, when Mark's wife Michelle walked into the room!

Breakfast done, we wandered outside for a smoke and to see the surroundings: The sky was blue and cloudless, the birds were singing, and the air was just so clean and fresh it almost seemed a pity to light a cigarette, but hell, when the habit's got you it's so hard to ignore. Sad but true.

Drew arrived at about eight thirty and we loaded our gear into the car, said our goodbyes to Mark and Michelle, and set off for Lands End. Full of anticipation and a certain amount of trepidation, we were fairly quiet on the journey, which took about an hour. On our arrival at Lands End, Drew parked the car (for free!!) and we filed dutifully, if a little raggedly to the signpost where everyone has their photo taken, and Drew explored the video camera until a young lady appeared and offered to take an "official" photo of us before we set off. Twenty four quid and five minutes later, at 10 on the dot, we said cheerio to Drew and set off, very high spirited along the South-West Coast Path. Of course, we had to take a look at the sea from the cliff top, and that was the moment when I realised how far down it was to the sea! It seemed as though we were airborne, the cliffs were so high! What a stunning view! We could see for what seemed like hundreds of miles. "Where are the Scilly Isles?", and "Is that Canada over there?"!

The scenery varies tremendously around Lands End, and we marvelled at the huge rugged granite cliffs dropping almost vertically to meet golden sands or to be engulfed by foaming waves. We followed the sandy path over bracken clad clifftops and hillocks dotted with gorse bushes towards Sennen Cove. Then we got lost!!! Well not really lost, you understand, we knew where we were, but the footpath had disappeared! Never mind, after a couple of minutes searching through the gorse and bracken we re-found the path, and followed our planned route, dropping down steeply through a small residential area, then up a minor road to the A 30. Trudging along the A 30 I phoned B.B.C. Radio Cornwall to try to arrange a bit of publicity, and to get any motorists in the area to recognise us and give us some audible encouragement. The lady I spoke to was very helpful, but either the presenter at that time did not get the message, or nobody in Cornwall listens to their local B.B.C. station!

About an hour along the A 30 we reached the wonderfully named village of Crows-an-Wra, where our route took us off the road and onto footpaths. Over a stile and into a field of the lushest, greenest grass you could imagine, the contrast from the road was like walking barefoot from sharp gravel onto a shagpile carpet! Only about a mile up the first footpath we stopped for a water and smoke break, and while we were leaning against a stone wall admiring the scenery I happened to glance skywards, and spotted a buzzard circling about half a mile away. As we watched, a second buzzard joined the first, and they circled together, gradually gaining height until they were little more than specks in the huge blue expanse of sky. I was getting more and more excited, and Neil and Mouse wondered what all the fuss was about, until I explained that, if my memory serves me right, during their mating rituals buzzards circle to a great height, and then lock their talons together and tumble, this being a test of the male bird's courage, to see how close to the ground they will get before he "bottles out" and lets go. I had never seen this spectacular display before, and as it turned out, I am still waiting!

The stupid birds made me strain my eyes, even though I was looking through binoculars, until they were nearly out of sight, and then disappeared in opposite directions! I guess I should have known that their mating season would have been over by May!

We carried on, across lush meadows divided by dry stone walls and through tiny farmyards, occasionally having to clamber over stiles, which were built into the dry stone walls, making friends with herds of cattle, (some of which made us a tad nervous!) as we went. We reached Sancreed at quarter past twelve, looking forward to a refreshing pint of lime and soda and a ploughmans lunch, or something similar, only to discover that the pub shown on the map had been closed for years. After consulting the map we decided to detour to a village called Madron (How dare they name a village after our mate Lovell!!), where at a pub called The King William IV, we devoured our lunch with (tomato) relish! Speaking to the Landlord, telling him the basics of what we were doing, we discovered that he has a daughter in Sittingbourne, no more than ten miles from our home village! As we finished our lunch the young chef/kitchen assistant came out and proffered a five pound note, explaining that it was from the Landlord. We thanked them both very much, then scrounged a large piece of paper from the pub, and a felt tip

Gez making friends with a herd of inquisitive cattle

pen, and wrote, as bold as we could, "LOVELL" on it so that when we came across the village sign on our way out of Madron we could take a picture of a sign saying "MADRON LOVELL"! You may have gathered by now that we have a friend called Ron Lovell. And he's mad.

From Madron we headed East, through Heamoor, along some beautiful lanes to Trevarrack, passing some wonderful little stone and slate cottages with Wisteria, Clematis and all sorts of other lovely fragrant creepers clinging to their walls. Keeping to the north of Penzance, we stuck to the tiny lanes before turning south, skirting the eastern edge of town. As we came to the brow of a hill, we knew we were getting close to the sea again, and as it came into sight, there was the beautiful view of St. Michaels Mount, sitting just off the coast to the east, and we headed straight for it and rejoined the South West Coast Path between Penzance and Marazion. By the time we reached the sea wall the wind had got up and was blowing straight off the sea into our right ears! And straight out of our left ears! The sea was just beginning to take notice of the wind, and the windsurfers and kite skiers were enjoying their sport, spending a lot of their time airborne, and quite a while in the drink as well! We slowed down considerably walking along the sea wall to Marazion, and decided to revive ourselves with a quick pint in the "Godolphin Hotel". I wish we hadn't bothered, as the beer was not the best. (No real ales!) We were supposed to be meeting Alison and Drew for a pint but they had been marooned on St. Michael's Mount, and got back too late. Never mind, we'd catch up later when we reached Goldsithney, our projected overnight stop.

We were much slower now we were nearing the end of the first day, but still comfortable with the day's mileage. We climbed out of Marazion following the main road, with the wind behind us all the way into Goldsithney where we arrived at half past five and went straight into the Trevelyan Arms to ask about B. & B. No joy there, so we went to the Guest House over the road and were greeted by a large sign saying "NO VACANCIES". Around the corner to another B. & B., once again, no vacancies, but at least this lady made a couple of phone calls, and sent us off in the right direction! Alison and Drew, and Drew's aunt Doreen met us in The Crown, and Drew took me to the B. & B., The Sunningdale (thanks for returning Neil's socks!) to unload our overnight gear and get a key, then we returned to The Crown for some more beer and social stimulation! Oh yes, we had some food as well. It didn't take very much, but we managed to drink the pub out of real ales that night! They are obviously not used to strangers turning up and drinking a couple of gallons! During the course of the evening we got talking to quite a few of the locals, and discovered that most of them aren't local at all! One guy, Pete McReedy, used to drink with Neil and Mouse in the Albion in Maidstone! This kind of encounter was to become a regular occurrence on our travels.

We returned to our B. & B. at about ten o'clock, picked our rooms, Neil and Mouse sharing a twin while I had the luxury of a single, showered and clambered into bed, feet and legs feeling okay, just generally tired after seven hours walking.

Monday 13th May. I arose at about twenty past seven, washed, dressed and made my way downstairs for breakfast, listening all the time to the sound of the rain lashing against the windows of the B. & B.. Mouse and Neil joined me in the dining room at just before eight o'clock, and we ate a full English breakfast looking gloomily out of the window at the slate grey sky, and hoping that there might be a break in the awful weather sooner rather than later! The Sunningdale was a very comfortable guest house, and to increase the comfort level for the majority of their guests they employ a no smoking policy, which meant that Neil and I would have to go outside for our routine morning fag! This we did, and wished we hadn't! The rain was driving into our faces whichever way we stood, impossible though that sounds, and we returned wet and demoralised to pack our gear up ready for when our support crew arrived.

Alison and Drew arrived at about nine, having been held up in traffic on the way. They were staying with Drew's aunt Doreen in Truro for the week, as it is about half way between Lands End and Fowey, where they were to hand over to the next support crew. Togged up in our waterproof suits we embarked on our second day's walk with heavy hearts. The weather was absolutely awful, the strong wind thrashing the rain against us, the more persistent droplets finding their way through to mingle with the sweat which inevitably starts as soon as we put our waterproofs on. To make things worse, there was no sign of a break in the clouds, and we were sure that we would be walking in rain for the rest of the day.

We stopped in the first village we came to, Trescowe, found a public phone box, (no reception on the mobile!) and I phoned Radio Cornwall to try to get some publicity, and having explained our situation I was gobsmacked when the woman on the other end of the phone said "If you could fax us the details of your route we may be able to do something"!!!!!! I had already explained to her that we were in the middle of nowhere in the pouring rain. Silly wench! Neil suggested that maybe we should have left the microwave oven and television set behind to make more room for the fax machine! Never mind, hopefully the people at Radio Cornwall will do something anyway.

We carried on across some stunning countryside, peering through the rain at the steep sided hills, the fields such a rich green that the battleship grey mist of persistent horizontal rain couldn't disguise it, all the way keeping to minor roads, as we realised that the footpaths would be very wet, through Nancegollan, and on to Porkellis where our lunch break was planned. Thankfully our lunchtime feeding and watering hole, The Star, was still open, perched on a hill with beautiful views across the patchwork panorama of the Cornish countryside, and we had a good lunch there, looking out of the windows watching the sky all the time as the cloud showed signs of breaking. The Landlord of the pub was from Belvedere, South East London, and knew where Lenham is, and kindly donated a fiver for our cause.

At last the rain stopped and we set off, still very damp, but now without waterproofs on, to head for Penryn, our anticipated overnight stop. Why is it that every hill we climb is longer and steeper than the downward slope on the other side?! We press on through the afternoon past Carnkie, along the hedged lanes to Polkanuggo, then onto the A 39 and into Longdowns, where we take a wrong turn and add about a mile to our journey, all on main roads. As we walked cheerfully down the A 39 just West of Penryn, Alison called my mobile phone to ask how we're getting on, and as she asked the question she answered it herself: "Whereabouts are you? Oh, there you are!". As they passed us tooting their horn, we all stuck our thumbs out but they carried on regardless!

When we reached Penryn, our anticipated overnight stop, we felt so sprightly that we decided to carry on to Falmouth. If you are a pessimist you would say that doing this added a mile or so to our day. The three of us are optimistic, and we say that it will take a mile or so off tomorrow's journey! Alison, Drew and Doreen met us in Falmouth, and as usual we headed for the pub, only this time we ordered a round of teas!! Drew and I then went to the Tourist Information office to enquire about B. & B. availability, found a guest house with vacancies, booked in, and returned to the pub to fetch Neil and Mouse. Drew then ferried us all to the B. & B. where the landlady made us welcome, informing us that her husband was away on business and wouldn't be back until the weekend! So we showered, changed, and .... yes, you guessed, we went to the pub! The taxi driver told us the best pubs in town, and we spent the entire evening drinking "Cornish Knocker" in The Chain Locker, just across the road from The Shipwrights. The two pubs have a reciprocal agreement whereby if they get too busy they recommend each other, which seems a sensible idea to me. It also makes good sense to the T-shirt printers. Three T-shirts printed with "THE CHAIN LOCKER & SHIPWRIGHTS" were donated by the Landlord, and were much appreciated!

During the evening we met a couple who seemed to be having trouble beating a quiz machine, and we decided to add our combined I Q to the task. Needless to say this brought winnings galore to the fortunate couple, who rewarded us with a pint each and the pleasure of their company for half an hour. After they left, our conversation degenerated and was terminated by Neil informing us that he felt that women whose eyes were slightly crossed (like Sophia Loren's, apparently!) gave the impression of being sexy, whereas women whose eyes looked slightly apart looked frighteningly insane! We laughed so much we had to order another beer! Then it was time for bed so we called a taxi and said our goodbyes to the staff, looking forward to a good night's sleep. However, the three of us wouldn't all fit into a double bed, so we drew lots and I slept on the floor, because I didn't fancy taking the landlady up on her hinted invitation!! Not the most comfortable night ever, but not too bad.

Tuesday 14th May. Up at seven, full breakfast, full of the joys of spring, looking forward to a long day's walk. The weather was looking good, sunny but with a strong wind chasing the grey and white fluffy clouds across the sky. Today was the day that had started our discussions on ease of walk versus scenery, and we had opted for the scenic route for a large proportion of the day. Drew met us at the B & B at ten past eight and took us to the harbour, (where our walk had ended the previous day) just in time to catch the eight thirty ferry from Falmouth to St. Mawes. The ferry was not quite what I had expected, quite small (i.e. minibus size) and just what you would have expected about half a century ago, brightly painted in blue and red, and with numerous white "spare tyres" suspended from the brilliant white handrail which ran all around the deck. Never mind, we're all swimmers! We boarded the ferry and after a quick chat with the Skipper to ensure a cheap (or even free!) voyage, we sat, none too comfortably on the upper deck until quarter past nine, when the second crew member turned up! Then we got under way, the little boat nosing its way out of the scattering of fishing boats moored at the quay, and out into the estuary of the River Fal, where the wind really woke us up!

We were now a little worried that the loss of three quarters of an hour at the beginning of the day would mean a late finish in Mevagissey, but there was nothing else for it but to get stuck in and try to make the time up en route.

The ferry docked in the picturesque village of St. Mawes at nine thirty, and we set off immediately up the steepest road we had come across so far. It was uphill for at least the first two miles, the gradient varying between about 1 in 3 and almost flat, and as we came to the ridge of the St. Just peninsular we were greeted with the most spectacular views back across the estuary to Falmouth and Penarrow Point (just to the north of Falmouth.). It seemed as though we had climbed thousands of feet, as the boats moored at Falmouth were now just colourful dots on the blue, brown and grey river, and the estuary seemed almost directly below us. We could see right out to sea, and up the split estuary which carries the Penryn River westwards, the River Fal northwards, and the Percuil River to the northeast. It was almost as though we were looking down on an aerial photograph!

Following the A 3078, (not by choice I hasten to add, it was just that the South West Coast Path would have taken us about 8 miles further!) we walked through St. Just in Roseland, until we reached a point just north-west of Trewithian, where we joined a footpath which would lead us to the South West Coast Path at the north-western side of Gerrans Bay. This path was reasonably level and dry, and we made good time in some very pleasant surroundings, hazel hedges and hawthorn and blackthorn sheltering us from the keen southerly wind. The views to the east here were almost as spectacular as the view I mentioned in the last paragraph back over to Falmouth. As we neared the cliffs on the eastern coast of the St. Just peninsula, we could hear the wind howling and the waves crashing at the foot of the cliffs. The only other sound was of seagulls crying plaintively, as if trying to warn us off!

We followed the Coast Path for about half a mile, up over some spectacular cliffs, which would have provided an ideal site for a school geography field trip, with their clearly defined layers of granite and clay, and with rusty splashes where the iron had come to the surface, then down the other side to the western end of Pendower beach, a long curved bay of golden sand.

We then cut inland following a beautiful stream valley, the bubbling crystal clear water looked so tempting, frolicking along the rocky stream bed. This peaceful valley was like a gorge, steep sided but easy walking for about two miles. As we climbed the western slope to come out of the valley, I noticed a tiny creature cowering near a large stone in the middle of the path. upon closer examination I saw it was a shrew, and it had obviously been attacked by some kind of predator, as it had a deep cut to the back of its head, possibly caused by a bird's talon? We will never know! We decided to leave it where it was and let Mother nature take her course, so we headed on up to the village of Veryan, where we revived ourselves with a quick pint of lime and soda each in a pub.

From Veryan we followed more footpaths and minor roads heading east to rejoin the South West Coast Path just south of Portloe. About a mile north along the coast, once again amongst superb scenery, the footpath following the ridge of the cliff, we skidded and skipped our way down the steep cliff path into Portloe. There we met Alison, Drew, and Doreen for lunch (yes, you guessed, in a pub again!), before continuing on our merry way north eastwards.

The Coast Path provided by far the most awesome scenery we had come across so far: Rugged beauty which defies description, but I'll try! The cliffs here were on more of a slope than any we had seen thus far, and slipped their way into the crashing sea at an angle of about 45 degrees. The sea was the colour of picture postcard seas from the more exotic parts of the world, you know, the ones that you get and say "The sea can't really be that colour, that must be computer enhanced!", and where it met the cliffs it boiled and foamed as though a huge vessel had been thrown into reverse! All manner of birds make their homes in such inhospitable places, and we saw cormorants, gulls, razorbills, fulmars, guillemots and many more which I struggled to identify. I wish I could

The view back past the picturesque village of Portloe.
The Coast Path runs along the ridge right at the centre of the picture.

hang in the sky like the gulls do, seemingly effortlessly, and then swoop at tremendous speed down to sea level before riding the thermals like an expert glider pilot to regain their original position. I might have seen more if I could have done that! I also wish there were more places to experience the silence and solitude which we found there.

The Coast Path seemed to cling on to the side of the cliffs, about half way up (or half way down, depending whether you're a pessimist or an optimist!), and consisted of an undulating six inch wide sandy rabbit track! And when I say "undulating" I mean to the tune of about five hundred feet every quarter of a mile! The terrain was the most difficult we had encountered, and we were all suffering aching legs and sore feet. The eight miles from Portloe to Mevagissey took us over four hours to walk, even though we cut inland for the latter stages, to try and keep to more level ground. The last mile, along a footpath from Galowras Mill through Penwarne to Mevagissey was more or less following the contour lines of the map, so was not hilly in the normal sense of the word, but meant that we were walking on a side-slope all the time, and although the scenery was lovely this was something we decided never to attempt again! The strain on the ankles and the sideways slipping of the feet in their boots was about the most uncomfortable part of the whole walk.

We reached Mevagissey at seven fifteen, meeting Alison and Drew as we dropped (almost literally!) into the village, and found ourselves a nice little boozer called The King's Arms, where we swiftly consumed the best pint of beer in the world. Well earned I reckon. Mouse was really suffering by now, from chest pains as well as leg and feet troubles. We were quite concerned about him for at least two minutes, until we realised that it hadn't affected his ability to quaff a pint in ten seconds or less!

I went and did my usual rounds attempting to find us some accommodation for the night, all to no avail. It seemed that there were no vacancies anywhere in Mevagissey, until we told the Landlord of the King's Arms of our plight. I think he took it as something of a personal challenge to find us somewhere, and after about two pints (mine not his!) he came over and told us he had found us somewhere to stay. Gratefully we ordered some food for an hour's time, and dragged our bags up the one in three incline to the B. & B. Bob had sorted for us, showered quickly and returned to the King's Arms for our dinner.

Almost as soon as we got there Mouse asked the Landlord if there would be any chance of a late drink! The answer, unsurprisingly, was an emphatic "NO"! So we ate our dinners, drank another beer or two, and did our best to ignore the winking and beckoning of the local "talent", a red headed desperado who was obviously suffering the effects of something more than just excess alcohol! She then came over to us, by now obviously aware that we were not going to go to her, and we made our excuses and went to explore the delights of Mevagissey (which we had by now renamed "Gisabevvy"!) Well, we went to another pub, anyway! At this quaint old harbourside pub I spotted a miniature barrel on the bar, with a tiny brass tap on the end over which was hung a sign proclaiming "Drunk in Cornwall, distilled in Hell"! My curiosity got the better of me and I asked the Landlord what it contained. He never actually gave us an answer, just telling us that it was from Jamaica (which gave us a fair clue!), but I can tell you it burnt like crazy on the way down, and gave me a lovely warm feeling in my stomach when it got there!

We made our way back to the King's Arms just before closing time and ordered one for the road, content now to sit quietly back and enjoy the atmosphere, supping slowly and contemplating our next day's walk, looking forward to a day's rest on the Thursday. That idea didn't last long. Bob, the Landlord decided to review his earlier decision, and at eleven fifteen, asked us if we would care to partake of another beer. Those of you who know us will realise just how silly a question that was! As the ale kept flowing, the Landlady, Geri, asked us if we knew any songs. Bob started us off with some Monty Python stuff, even going to the trouble of going out to his computer room and printing the words for us so we could sing along! We carried on with The Engineer's Song, I Don't Want To Join The Army, and a few others gradually degenerating until they became so filthy we almost embarrassed ourselves! Anyway, after about the fifth, at about one thirty, we wobbled our way wearily back up the one in three hill to our B & B. Needless to say, we slept well that night. The decision as to whether Mouse could carry on or not was to be discussed in the morning. I think we all knew what the verdict would be.

Wednesday 15th May. The smell of bacon, eggs and toast woke me at seven forty five, and my head woke shortly afterwards, trying to piledrive its way down through my neck!! A quick wash and brush-up later, I was in the dining room trying to scrounge some painkilling pills (enough for three!) from the boss-man. Neil and Mouse were not far behind me, and the decision was taken that Mouse should get a lift with Alison and Drew to try and see a Doctor about his chest pains, and either rejoin us for the next day's walking, (which would be Friday), or catch a train home, depending on the Doctor's advice. The pains that Mouse was suffering were worrying me more now, as they curtailed his hunger to the point that he could only manage his own breakfast, and didn't try to scrounge any of ours!! And a marvellous breakfast it was. Is it a genetic thing that makes men the best breakfast cooks?!

Alison and Drew met us at nine forty five and agreed to take Mouse to Fowey to find a surgery, before spending the rest of their day holidaying with Doreen, so Neil and I set off at nine fifty, climbing one of the steepest hills we had so far encountered to get out of Mevagissey.

We had decided to alter our route today, and take the easiest route to Fowey, instead of following the South West Coast Path, as we feared that the rough terrain of the coastal path two days on the trot might be too strenuous for us, so having climbed north out of Mevagissey we followed

The beautifully flat(!) Pentewan Valley Trail to the north of Mevagissey

minor roads to Pentewan, where we joined the Pentewan Valley Trail. This trail follows the St. Austell River valley, heading almost directly north, and despite the fact that it is always close to the B 3273 (the main route from St. Austell to Mevagissey), it is quiet and, thankfully, almost dead flat! We marched on up the valley, all the time keeping a look out for fish in the river, (not that we were hungry, just that we are both interested in fish!), through some lovely woods, with the shadows playing games of hide and seek with the leaves on the trees, and the river playing tunes to our sense of thirst, until we reached Tregorrick, where we turned right onto minor roads again, heading for Charlestown. This brought us back onto the more hilly roads, and Neil and I decided that somebody with great influence on nature had reorganised gravity to be relevant to us rather than sea-level! It seemed that every day our walking took us up about five thousand feet, but only down one thousand! Yet we always finished at sea level! At this rate we should meet some aircraft soon! Having climbed a few small hills and gone down one or two tiny ones, still in beautiful surroundings, with cheery Cornish folk growling or squeaking their greetings to us as we stomped along through their lovely county, we arrived in Charlestown.

What a beautiful little place, all stone walls and slate roofs, hanging baskets and climbing plants. As we rounded a corner to walk down towards the harbour we were greeted by the sight of six masts of varying height, some fully rigged with little monkey-like figures clambering around them, others stripped to the bare mast, towering above the slate roofs of the cottages surrounding a dry dock in the harbour where two tall ships were undergoing renovation. We spent a while walking round the dock, taking photographs and admiring the view, and marvelling at the workmanship of the teams scurrying around replacing hull timbers and mast seatings etc. until eventually the Pier House Hotel beckoned us in for lunch, and a very good lunch it was. Then it was back onto the Coast Path to head east towards Par and Fowey.

The South West Coast Path to the east of Charlestown is not quite so challenging, and we enjoyed the relatively gentle climb up onto the cliffs, along well maintained paths and still with some lovely scenery to view. However, about a mile and a half from Charlestown we came across what we now know to be "The Cornwall Coliseum". This monstrous construction is a disgrace to a beautiful county. Set on a mile long stretch of what used to be beautiful golden sand, with near hundred foot cliffs to the north and the English Channel to the south, this massive concrete and steel complex is a real eyesore and is visible from a fair distance either way along the coast path. All this destruction of a natural haven for a nightclub and concert venue!! I was lost for words when a local man told us what it was. Cornwall County Council, and St. Austell Borough Council should hang their heads in shame, having allowed this stretch of coastline to be ruined forever. Anyway, back down off my soap-box now!

We carried on across the cliffs and golf courses to Par, (I reckon there are more golf courses in Cornwall than there are golfers!) where we dropped a few feet back down to sea level, and followed the S. W. Coast Path around a huge chemical factory with its own dock, where an ocean going ship was being unloaded by huge vacuum pumps, before walking through the village, comfortable in the knowledge that it was only three and a half miles into Fowey. That three and a half miles must have been measured in a dead straight line! Not even as the crow flies! There were not only hills in the way, there were corners to go round whichever way we went, and we reckon it was a misprint on the sign, and it should have said five and a half miles! Never mind, we made it in the end.

We met Alison, Drew, Doreen and Mouse near the "Visitor Centre" where they had parked the car, and walked down the steep, narrow streets into Fowey centre, while Mouse told us about his visit to the Doctor. The news was not good. The Doctor had told him that he must not continue the walk, as he suspected the problem was angina. It turned out that for some considerable time Mouse had known that he had a problem, but had not said anything because he had not wanted to let us down! I'm just glad that the problem had not manifested itself when we were on the Coast Path, miles from anywhere!

After a quick chat, for once with no beer involved, we decided that Drew would take Mouse and myself back to Par, to unload the bags from the car, and drop Mouse at the railway station to make his way home, then Drew would return to Fowey to collect Alison, Doreen and Neil. On the way to Par I phoned the number I had been given to arrange to collect the keys to the Methodist Church hall where we would be staying. We were met at the Church hall by Morag, who gave me the keys, and a brief guided tour of the Church and hall, warned me that in the morning we might be woken by the local ladies Yoga class, before she dashed off to prepare an evening meal for her husband, Nick. Nick was the local representative of N.C.H., and had kindly offered the Church Hall as accommodation for two nights.

I said my goodbyes to Mouse, and Drew took him off to catch his train. I then retired to the pub just down the road, which didn't look much from the outside, and it seemed that outside was the only view I was going to get for a while! This was the only pub we had seen on our way through Par. Neil and the others turned up about 10 minutes before opening time to find me sitting outside with my tongue hanging out bemoaning the fact that civilisation (as in all day opening!) had not yet reached this far flung corner of our glorious land! The pub was called The Welcome Home, and seemed to be the only licensed establishment for miles, so we waited a few minutes, and hey presto, the doors opened. In we went to be greeted by a good selection of beers, and a landlady from - - - - - - - - - - you guessed it, Kent! The Welcome Home was a pleasant little pub with a friendly atmosphere, and it taught us never to judge a book by its cover. Alison and Drew and Doreen had a quick drink with us and said goodbye, as this was the last day of their stint as our support crew. Neil and I stayed on for another beer or two, (or four), then made our way back to the Methodist Church Hall for a wash and change before resuming maintenance of our alcohol levels!

Although we were grateful for the accommodation provided at the Church Hall, we had not thought about the lack of washing facilities! Now it's not that we're shy or anything, but we were distinctly ill at ease stripping off and washing our sweaty parts in the kitchen of the Church Hall! Not only did it seem somehow irreverent, it was not exactly private. However, there seemed to be no other choice, so there we stood, as nature had made us, in front of a plate glass window, with the lights on (as it was now the wrong side of dusk) looking out at a row of terraced cottages, hoping that the local Convent didn't decide to take their constitutional there and then! Laugh? We nearly did!

After a quick wash and brush up I phoned a taxi to take us to Fowey, so that we could suss out the lie of the land for tomorrow's day off. The cab driver spent the journey regaling us with stories of his exploits and conquests in Fowey, and telling us which pubs to visit and which to steer clear of, so as we arrived in the town centre we thanked him very much, and ignored every word of his advice! First stop was The Ship Inn, ("steer clear of that one, that's a trouble spot" the man had said). What a wonderful place! Good beer, an extensive menu, and a vibrant atmosphere stemming from the landlord and his staff. One member of his staff was of immense interest to Neil. Young Aimee had made an immediate impression, and I thought for a while that I might have to complete the rest of the walk on my own! Neil seemed to be oblivious to anything I said, and by the end of the evening had even managed to perfect a mechanical movement to convey his beer jug from table to mouth while never taking his eyes off her!!

As we stood at the bar, toward the end of a very pleasant evening, explaining to the boss and barmaids what we were doing there, a voice from behind us asked "Did you say Lenham?". We turned around to see two chaps, obviously fairly inebriated, one considerably more so than the other, leaning back in their chairs grinning inanely at us. Just as I was thinking "Oh, no, I don't want to get involved in a conversation with these two.", Neil stopped me in my tracks! "Hallo mate!! Blimey, it's been a few years since I've seen you! Do you remember me? I rebuilt your Jag. for you back in the seventies!" It turned out that he had indeed rebuilt this fellow's Jag, when he had lived in Maidstone, but the resultant conversation was more entertaining than big ends and track rods! Or track ends and big rods, come to that! The stories that came out that evening about some of the tricks that used to be played in and around Maidstone's pubs, the bands that used to play local gigs, and the cars that were lovingly maintained, hand painted, then crashed, nearly made my hair curl! James, the ex Jag owner, now lives in Cornwall with Quentin, who we at first thought was his son, but now know to be his "significant other half". Quentin was slaughtered, having been drinking red wine all evening, and became very jealous of his "other half" being "chatted up" by two slightly more "butch" guys. I said guys, not gays!!!! As Quentin staggered off in the general direction of the toilets, James decided it was time to go home. So we carried on chatting to him about what we were doing and why we were doing it, in the hope that some kind of monetary donation would be forthcoming. Our hopes were in vain! Twenty minutes later he decided that it would be a good idea to retrieve Quentin from the Gents' toilet before he went home! All the time we had been talking to these two guys (check for misprint) the landlord and his staff were in stitches, and when eventually it was time to go, we were offered another drink, on the house. Well, it would have been rude to refuse, wouldn't it, so after ensuring that Aimee would be there tomorrow, we called a taxi, which duly arrived at 2345 hours and took us back to our "home" for the night.

Take my word for it, after four days hard walking the last place you will want to sleep is on a parquet floor, with only a sleeping bag between you and the wooden blocks! However, we had anaesthetised ourselves pretty well over the course of the evening, and we now know that tomorrow is going to be a good day. The conversation was pretty limited, mostly words of one syllable, and punctuated by giggles and grunts and groans as we turned over and over trying to find a comfortable position in which to sleep! I guess we must have got to sleep at some point though, because the next thing I remember was waking up!!

Chapter 2

A Day in Fowey

We awoke at 8.30 to have a wash and a cup of tea before the ladies' yoga class started. As it was, we were too late, they had already arrived and set up, so we pulled on some clothes, thankful that we had had the chance to wash the previous evening, and went to the local shop to see what they could offer us for breakfast. The weather was looking reasonable, sunny with a few small white clouds chasing each other across the blue, and the first thought that went through our minds as we wandered lazily to the shop was how nice it was to be relieved of the pressure of the last few days. No deadlines to meet, no decisions to take as to which route to take, and , best of all, no distance to walk today! At the shop we again had cause to rue the lack of "civilisation" in this corner of England.: There were no sandwiches on the shelves, and our enquiries revealed no cafe in Par, so we made do with a Cornish pasty and a bottle of fruity drink followed by a chocolate bar. What a wonderfully healthy breakfast!

Back at the Church Hall we went in the front entrance to introduce ourselves to the girls in the yoga class, and explain the coffee cups (washed up, I hasten to add!) on the draining board in the kitchen. We came to the conclusion that Cornwall must indeed be "God's country" as we kept being told, as all the "girls" attending the yoga class were at least sixty years old, and the oldest we learned was eighty four! If I am supple enough to perform those kind of contortions when I'm fifty I shall consider myself fortunate! As the ladies drifted off, some of them insisting on leaving donations for our walk on the way, Neil and I got down to the business of washing and changing into half decent clothes, and mentioned the necessity to get some smalls washed today. Once dressed, we scouted around outside the Hall to try and find somewhere to hang our washing out to dry, and finding no possible places, we gave up on that idea and called a taxi to take us to Fowey!

The taxi arrived at exactly 12 noon and the driver informed us that Fowey was holding the Daphne du Maurier festival this week, and we should have a good time today. As if we needed an excuse to have a good time!!! When he discovered that I was a Town Crier and that we were meeting the Fowey Town Crier, the driver also told us that he knew Michael Penprase (the Fowey Town Crier), and that he should make our day even more enjoyable! I was beginning to think that somebody was on our side after all!!!

We arrived in Fowey and carted all my gear into the Ship Hotel, where, as we had arranged, I changed in an upstairs staff room, while Neil had a quick pint, (and a chat with Aimee!) and we went out to explore the town. Fowey is one of the loveliest little towns I have ever visited, all steep hills and tiny little streets, characterful cottages and beaming people. Michael had told me that he would not be able to meet us until about 3 o'clock that afternoon, and as I was unsure of the etiquette of Town Crying in somebody else's domain, I kept quiet. This turned out to be a good thing, as we were approached by numerous people asking what we were doing, and with Neil bearing "The Hat", we collected £60 in half an hour, never more than about 200 yards from the pub, and without even exercising the vocal chords! Good start or what?

Back in The Ship we ordered lunch, along with the essential beer, and chatted with the Landlord and his staff while we awaited the arrival of our food. I had ordered a chilli-con-carne, as I like to give my vocal chords a bit of a challenge, and Neil ordered the same. We had just about finished sweating our way through our meals when in walked Mike. He actually arrived well before 3 o'clock, and it was clear from the moment he walked in that we were going to get along just fine. The Landlord knew him well enough to have his beer pulled before he reached the bar, and as he offered us one each as well, we realised that this might be quite a long session! Mike then proceeded to take us on a guided tour of his beloved town. This was when the fun really started!

Mike's outfit is a rich russet-brown colour, with plenty of gold braid, and several badges from competitions he has taken part in, and has been around the block a few times! (A bit like Mike really!!). We walked out of The Ship, and straight across the street, with Mike greeting all and sundry as if he knew them all, which he probably did, down a very narrow side street, and came out at a lovely Promenade on the estuary of the River Fowey. The whole area of flagstone paved, split level almost patio like riverside was encircled by well maintained wrought iron railings which, as well as offering safety, added a sense of envelopment to the promenade. Looking out over the water to Polruan was where the quaint glory of the town really came out. The estuary was alive with boats of all shapes, sizes, colours and designs, some moored awaiting their next expedition, some busy ferrying people across the river to Polruan, and some larger vessels transporting goods up the river to the commercial quays. There were quite a few people there, mostly sightseers, and Michael introduced me as the Town Crier of - - - - - - - - - - "where is it you're from?" - - - - - - - - - - "Oh yes, Lenham!" I then proceeded to let everybody in Fowey know exactly who we were, where we were from, and what we were doing disrupting their peaceful afternoon in this wonderful little town. Neil again worked wonders with "The Hat", and we adjourned after about half an hour to lubricate the operative parts!

For this very necessary lubrication Mike took us to a pub just round the corner from The Ship, the name of which I have no chance of remembering. All will become clear! Having ordered a pint in this second pub, after no more than five minutes Mike deposited his empty jug on the table, and said "Come on then, we haven't got all day! There are another twelve pubs in town to do yet!". Neil and I broke the habit of a lifetime then. We discussed for a moment the virtues of remaining sober for at least another couple of hours, and left our beer on the table outside, right on the pavement, following Mike along the road to the next Ale House. You must forgive me, but my recollection of the following events is a little hazy!

He took us into the shop where his wife works, and introduced us to her (I'm ashamed to say I can't remember her name), then rushed us out to the next pub before we dried out too much(!!!), a quick pint in there, and off to show us the "Saints' House". The front of this imposing building is absolutely beautiful, and is marked as a Saints' House by a large cockle shell design above the front door. My knowledge of architecture is not good, (sorry Dad!) but I think the building is Georgian. I mentioned that we had walked part of The Saints' Way as we came into Fowey, and Mike told us that these Saints' Houses are dotted along the entire length of The Saints' Way, originally used as shelters for the Pilgrims on their way to Winchester. What he didn't tell us was how many there were, or how long the path is. (Well, I don't recall him telling us, anyway!). Enough of the history lesson(?!), time to thin down the blood with some more alcohol. Oh no, I think I'm going to fall over!

We visited another couple of pubs in the town centre, and then we revisited the one where we had left our beer. there was our beer, just where we had left it, a little warmer now, but still perfectly drinkable! I think I could have left my wallet there without losing it! After we had had a short interlude to finish our beer Mike started to lead us out of the harbour area, where we had been all this time, and up a steep hill, (just what we wanted!) towards where we had met Alison and Drew, yesterday. Only we turned off before I could get my bearings properly, so now I was well and truly lost!

We went into The Royal Fowey Yacht Club, met a few quite generous millionaires, drank a large Bacardi and Coke each, then made our way still further up the side of the cliff (or so it seemed) to The Royal Fowey Hotel, where we met a few more millionaires, a few superstars, actors, actresses, singers, musicians, and a wonderful barman

Gez making his presence heard in Fowey, accompanied by Michael Penprase, Town Crier of Fowey

who agreed to serve me a shandy, instead of the headbanging beer that Mike was trying to get me to drink! It was then that Mike told us that this was where the Daphne du Maurier Festival was happening. That explained quite a lot. I had thought for a while that we'd walked all the way to Hollywood!!

We saw two of the Nolan sisters, lovely little things about navel height, a wrinkly old fellow who Neil told me was Dave Berry, an actress by the name of Helen Wier, and Brian Poole of The Tremeloes! Wow, we were really hob-nobbing with the stars! We spent about a quarter of an hour in the hotel and then walked a couple of hundred yards further up the hill to the tented village where all the real festivities were happening. After a while Mike said he was going to have to leave us, and as we would have had no chance of finding our own way back to Fowey town centre, we left with him and he pointed the way from where he lived. We wobbled our (very) merry way back to The Ship in town arriving at about eight-thirty and set about counting the money we had collected, making sure that it didn't get confused with our beer money! We ate some dinner (I can't remember what we had!), then I changed back into "civvies" and we had another beer, just for a change! I expect most of you will have heard the phrase "drink yourself sober", and that is exactly what Neil and I did that evening.

As we sat chatting to each other about the next day, and what we could expect on the Coastal Path, a group of people came in who we had spoken to earlier in the day. They were a group of travelling actors and actresses who come every year to the Daphne-du-Maurier festival, and they had just finished their day's performance, and were looking forward to a well earned drink. Then I saw her. A Marilyn Monroe lookalike who swayed elegantly to the table, and slid gracefully into a chair as if she was slipping into a bathful of champagne! I told Neil that I was going to introduce myself, and stood, a little uncertainly I feel, and walked (or wobbled!) over to where the group had sat themselves. A couple of the guys recognised me and said hello, and after returning their greetings I turned to face the object of my drunken desire. As I gazed (or should that be "glazed"?) into her face, my attention was drawn to her eyes. You remember the conversation about eyes that we had had in Falmouth? This was the example that had been sent to me as a lesson! One eye looked at me, the other looked about 30 degrees to my left, straight at the bar! I was lost for words. Those of you who know me may not believe that, but I assure you, it's true. I did eventually manage to utter some inane babble about the remarkable likeness to Marilyn Monroe, and I don't think I upset her too much, but it taught me a lesson. Don't open the book until you've looked at the cover!! I felt awful about my intrusion into their group and my subsequent embarrassing silence, but they all soon made me feel comfortable and we had a bit of "proper" conversation before I returned to my walking buddy Neil.

At about nine-thirty a familiar face presented itself in front of me and I immediately thought it was Lyn Hollier, the likeness was incredible, but what would she be doing in Cornwall at this time of year? Oh yes, she and husband Phil were our next support team!!! They had been trying to call my mobile 'phone all day to find out where we were going to be, but as mobile phones don't work in Fowey, they couldn't get through. When we had spoken last, which had been the previous evening, I had said that we would probably be in the Ship, but I hadn't explained exactly where the Ship was, and they had spent the last hour in the Ship just outside Par waiting for us to come in. After that hour, Phil had realised that something was not right, and they eventually came and found us. Just as well really, because we were in no fit state to go and find them! They had a quick chat and a beer and I described as best I could where we wanted them to meet us in the morning, gave them the money we had collected, (£310!!!) and they disappeared to their B & B, obviously tired after a long journey down from Kent. (I believe that Phil had already done a day's work before they left, so he must have been exhausted.)

At ten o'clock I called the local taxi company to take us back to Par, and was dismayed to be told there were no cars available until eleven-thirty! Oh dear, more beer! We spent the remainder of a fantastic evening in the company of some lovely people, and were quite sad when closing time came, and then our taxi arrived. We got back to the Church Hall in Par at 1145, not particularly looking forward to the unyielding floor which was to be our mattress for the night, but then we had a brainwave! I can't remember which one of us thought of it, but we decided to borrow all the hassocks (the softish things that you kneel on in Church), and use them as mattresses! Then we had second thoughts. We shouldn't abuse the hospitality afforded to us by the Church, so we'd suffer the hard floor for one more night. Then we changed our minds again, deciding that God would rather see us get a good night's sleep and continue our walk in more comfort the next day, so we scuttled into the Church proper, collected all the hassocks we could find, and made a swift exit, as though we were naughty boy scouts or something! The hassocks provided a much more comfortable mattress than the bare floor, and although I must admit I have spent more comfortable nights under canvas, I did sleep fairly well.

Chatting for a while before we went to sleep, we both said how much we were looking forward to getting back on the road in the morning. Strange how you can look forward to something which you know is going to cause you so much pain!!

Chapter 3

Fowey to Exmouth

Friday 17th May. We arose slightly later than anticipated, at about 0830, heads a little sore but full of memories of the previous day's debauchery, and with every intention of revisiting Fowey at the earliest opportunity. We had a quick wash, and had just about got dressed by the time Lyn and Phil turned up, followed by Nick, the N.C.H. rep, who wished us luck for the rest of our journey and retrieved the Church hall keys before dashing off to work. Lyn fussed around us like we were a pair of kids, and didn't even bat an eyelid when we thrust two steaming bags of sweaty clothing at her to take to the launderette! Phil drove us to Fowey to restart the walk from the point where we had finished on Wednesday evening, and Lyn told us not to hesitate to call them on their mobile if we needed anything on our way to Crafthole, where we planned to spend the night in accommodation kindly arranged by Nick on behalf of N.C.H..

We had a marvellous breakfast in a little cafe just round the corner from The Ship, before catching the 1015 ferry across the River Fowey to Polruan. The ferry was even smaller and older than the one we had experienced in Falmouth, but at the same time, it was a much shorter journey, so we weren't too bothered!

No time to explore Polruan, although it looks a lovely little village, we headed straight up the only road into (and therefore out of!) the little fishing port, up a 1 in 4 hill which went on for about a mile! Then we were back onto the S.W. Coastal Path, and the going got a bit easier. The Coastal Path seemed to keep to the same altitude for quite a distance, winding its way in and out of the coves and headlands past Blackbottle

Rock, around Lantic Bay to Pencarrow Head, all names that play with the imagination, and provide some exceptional scenery inland, as well as the terrific views out over the English Channel.

However, once we passed Pencarrow Head the terrain once more threatened to force us to divert from our planned route, in favour of the easier roads which ran close by. We are now certain that before long we will meet a Jumbo or a Concorde heading for New York! Altitude sickness hasn't been a problem so far, but it surely won't be long! We discussed the situation and decided to persevere with the Coastal Path and see how we felt when we reached Polperro. So on we went, around Lantivet Bay, passing the aptly named "Shag Rock" where Neil said "Doesn't look very comfortable for a shag!" Then I explained that a shag is a seabird similar to a cormorant, just like the one sitting on the outcrop right then, and it all made sense to him! Well, you can't go leaving people in confusion forever now, can you.

Although the Coastal Path was very hard going, when we reached Polperro we decided that it was worth the effort to gain the views and avoid the traffic, so after a short touristy nose around the tiny streets of the village we took off again, up onto the cliffs with the deep blue of the English Channel on our right, and the varying colours of the cliffs, dotted with clinging shrubs, and clumps of grass to our left, occasionally as we reached the top of a cliff, we'd peer over to see a valley sliding away inland to be met by the foot of a hill which reminded us of the views of the North Downs with which we are so familiar, and which, at this point, are so far away.

The weather was beginning to look decidedly dodgy now, and with the wind helping us on our way, we pressed on along the clifftops and as we rounded a headland about halfway between Polperro and Looe we saw a heap of rocks about half a mile out to sea, being pounded by the huge waves which had had nothing to stop them gaining momentum all the way across the Atlantic Ocean. The sight was spectacular, and one I'll never forget; it looked like one of the scenes out of a nautical movie. The spray coming off the waves as they crashed against the little islands was heaving itself right up over the top of the rocks, which, looking at the map now, I can tell you are 47 metres high at their highest point! Awesome.

As we approached Looe from the south, along the Coastal Path, we looked down onto huge grey-brown slabs of granite laid in parallel lines along the coast. Nature has an incredible knack of being more perfect than human endeavour could ever hope for! These granite slabs stretched for hundreds of yards, seemingly separated by no more than inches in places, but each slab being at least 5 yards across. They looked as though they had been laid by a giant kerb layer!

We rounded the headland just to the south of Looe, and dropped steeply into the town, stopping at a pub on the western side of the estuary for lunch and the inevitable pint of lime and soda, then crossing the river at the only bridge for miles and heading south again to the coast. The weather was still pretty rough, and we took the decision to follow the Coastal Path to Millendreath, then take the minor road into Seaton, as this would not add any distance to the walk, the road running parallel to the coast. This last section of the day's walk was the most tiring, and we struggled our way on along the Coastal Path then the road into Seaton and decided to call Phil and Lyn to come and meet us. After a cup of tea in a little cafe on the eastern side of the Seaton valley, we headed on along the coast road, meeting Lyn and Phil after we had climbed to the top of a very steep hill, which we could have done without! We gratefully eased our aching limbs into the car, and then discovered that it was all downhill to Crafthole!

We all agreed that that day's walk was a lot further than I had anticipated, and when we reached the house where we were to spend the night we found out that the owner of the house was an ex- R.A.F. air-sea rescue man, and he had spent the last couple of years of his service surveying the South West Coastal Path, and what he didn't know about it really wasn't worth knowing. He estimated that we had walked nearer 35 miles than the 21-22 planned, all due to the altitude variations of the coast path. No wonder we were knackered!

After a quick wash and change, we spent a very pleasant evening in The Finnygook pub. Strange name, stranger pub! It was quite an old building, but had been extensively modernised and refurbished inside, and came over as a bit characterless. Strange for a pub with a name that conjures up all kinds of images of Cornish smuggling and devilry! Still, the food was good, and the beer o.k.. We sat there chatting with Lyn And Phil until about ten o'clock before making our way back to our hosts' house for a well earned night's sleep. We had to decline the kind offer of tea or coffee, and I went to bed feeling slightly guilty that we had spent so little time acquainting ourselves with these kind people.

They had shown a great deal of interest in what we were doing, and we couldn't even be bothered to spend half an hour telling them about it. I will make sure that they get a free copy of this when it's finished.

Saturday 18th May. We came to at about quarter past seven on the Saturday morning, after the most comfortable night's sleep so far, to the smell of yet another fry-up being prepared for our benefit! Phil and Lyn arrived just as we finished our breakfast, having spent the night at a bed and breakfast a little way away, and we thanked our hosts for looking after us, loaded up and got in the car to make our way back to yesterday's finishing point, which we reached at half past eight. The weather seemed to have taken a turn for the better, the wind having dropped, and the sky looking much more friendly, and we started the day in good spirits, walking back past where we had just come from, the gentle breeze on our backs just encouraging us along. The scenery was not so spectacular now, but just as pleasant, with gentle slopes of green and brown, the occasional flock of sheep scattering as we approached or herd of cows being nosey and investigating us, but as we neared Plymouth Sound the sheer scale of the expanse of water surprised me. I had never realised quite how big the Tamar Estuary is. It seemed like miles and miles of slate blue and black water just being gently ruffled by the now feeble breeze. The motionless huge grey warships at anchor in the Sound and up the estuary towards Devonport docks seemed to be bored, just waiting for their call up to transform them into super-fast killer sharks.

We walked through Millbrook village, and out past the mud flats which at high water become Millbrook Lake, around the edge of Mount Edgecumbe Country Park, and into Cremyll, from where the ferry was to take us to Plymouth. Lo and behold, just behind the ferry docking point was a pub. And it was open! In we walked, depositing our webbing belts which carried our water bottles, waterproofs, maps etc., on the floor and ordering a pot of tea for two, with biscuits, and ensuring that it would be served in time to catch the next ferry. We relaxed for about twenty minutes sipping our tea and munching our biscuits, and enjoying the view out over the narrows to Devil's Point, safe in the knowledge that we wouldn't miss the ferry as we would be able to see it coming back across the estuary to Cremyll.

Once on the ferry, having secured a free crossing, we sat back to admire the scenery. Then I realised I'd left my waterproof hat in the pub!

Never mind, we were under way by the time I realised, so I would have to do without for the rest of the walk. It was no big deal, as we had waterproof hoods on our coats anyway, it was just the sentimental value of a hat which had kept my head dry for many years, all over the country, and it now looked as though it was about to rain!

Once in Plymouth, we looked at the map to decide which would be the most scenic route through the city. I don't know if you've ever been to Plymouth, but from what we saw there is no way any of it could be described as scenic! The first couple of hundred yards, from the ferry dock through the old naval barracks was probably the best part of Plymouth! The rest of it just seemed grey! I'm sure a lot of people will disagree, but I can only comment on what we saw, and most of it was modern, concrete shopping malls, and with the rain now starting to fall it just seemed GREY! We stopped in the doorway of a Church and donned our waterproofs, hoping that the rain wouldn't last too long, and by the time we had walked another quarter of a mile the sun was shining again! So we disrobed and chose the most direct route, and headed out of town as fast as our legs would carry us! Of course, as soon as we had stowed our waterproofs away the clouds reappeared, but we suffered a couple of very short showers without resorting to the horrible sweaty constricting nylon again. We reached the Marsh Mills area, right on the nort-eastern outskirts of town, at a quarter to two, and thought it was time for lunch, so we found The Marsh Mills pub, a Beefeater, and ordered our usual lime and sodas, and some Pasta in a tomato and herb sauce. The Landlord came over to us after a couple of minutes, and we thought for a moment he was going to ask us to leave. We must have been a bit off-putting to other customers, dressed in army combat trousers and with none too fresh sweat stains on our T-shirts, but he was just inquisitive as to what we were doing. So we told him, and our lunch was free! Very much appreciated, and not only by the pocket. It really gives you a buzz when somebody shows their appreciation like that, and we hadn't seen much of it that day, so it really gave us a lift for the afternoon's walk.

As we set off after lunch, heading for Ivybridge, we knew there was a fair chance of losing our way, because when I had bought the maps to plan the route, there was a small gap of about 3 miles for which I thought a £6.95 map was unnecessary. It may have saved us a couple of hours, as it turned out, but what the Hell, it wouldn't have been so much fun, would it?!

After consultation with the next map, and agreeing which town to head for, Neil and I found our way to the A 3416, which should have taken us to Langage Cross, nearly a mile north of the A 38. However, the road signs confused us and we ended up on the A 38, still heading in the right direction, towards Ivybridge, but on a very busy road instead of a tiny narrow lane. The A 38 is a dual carriageway, and has no footpath alongside it, so we were forced to scramble our way along the grass verges or risk our necks walking on the cycle lane (about two feet wide) which most of the motorists seemed to think was a piece of road to be used when the main carriageway got too boring! It's a shame we missed our route because from what we could see of it, the scenery would have been very good, looking north towards the southern edge of Dartmoor, where the clouds were now just hiding the tops of the hills.

As we walked through a cutting about three miles outside Ivybridge, we saw a Badger at the side of the road, totally indifferent to the traffic no more than a few feet away roaring by at 70 miles per hour plus. It didn't even move as we passed by, about two feet away. Now, most of you will know that Badgers are normally very shy creatures, and some of you may even have guessed that this one was dead! But it answered our questions as to what the evil smell was that we had been experiencing for the last quarter of a mile!

We carried on along the A 38 to Lee Mill, and from there took less busy roads the last couple of miles into Ivybridge, (not the quiet roads that we had hoped for, but less busy than the A 38) passing some quaint picturesque cottages on the way, meeting Lyn and Phil as we entered the town centre. They had organised a Bed and Breakfast for us, and we were only a couple of hundred yards from it, so the usual shower and change later, there we were ready to hit the town!

So off we went in search of beer, food and entertainment of some description, into town, a quick pint in a pub which didn't serve food, then another quick pint in the same pub because the beer was good! Then off to find a bit of grub. The next pub we came to looked a bit rough, but we decided to give it a try anyway. We had been right, it was a bit rough. And they didn't serve food either! Asking around, we discovered that there was no curry house, a dodgy chinky, a very expensive Italian restaurant, or "you could try The Duke of Cornwall" which we had passed on our way into town! So we did. And we're glad we did! After perusing the menu for a while, Lyn opted for the Seafood Platter, while Phil, Neil and I chose the mixed grill. Or should that have been "MIXED GRILL!"? Served on huge carving platters, the Mixed Grill consisted of a 6 oz. Steak, a lamb chop, a pork chop, 2 pieces of liver, 2 kidneys, 2 rashers of back bacon and a jumbo sausage!!! Then came the vegetables: A huge bowl of chips, an equally huge bowl of roast potatoes, a slightly smaller bowl of potato gratin, and more normal sized bowls of carrots. broccoli and cabbage. Lyn's Seafood Platter was almost as big, and she got more vegetables with hers!! Needless to say we spent the rest of the evening in The Duke of Cornwall, a) because it was such a nice pub, and b) because we couldn't move! What a wonderful meal!

We got back to the B. & B. at about quarter past ten, and after a quick smoke Neil and I discussed the day's walk. It had been the easiest twenty odd miles we had experienced so far, but the scenery had been the worst, and we had become quite bored walking through Plymouth and along the main roads, so we decided that in future, if a choice had to be made between scenery and ease of walk, the scenery would win every time. Then I discovered that after a large meal Neil snores!

Sunday 19th May. Awoke at about seven-thirty to be told by Neil that after a heavy meal I snore! Had a leisurely breakfast with Lyn and Phil, loaded the car, arranging to call them at lunchtime, and set off at ten to nine through Ivybridge town centre. It was a grey and misty morning, and our planned route was up into the southern edge of Dartmoor, then east to South Brent. As the mist was getting heavier, we bottled out and stuck to the minor roads through Bittafford, then rejoining our planned route at South Brent. It seemed that no matter how we planned things, the weather made us change our minds. There seemed little point in taking the scenic route in mist that was rapidly turning to fog!

The weather forecast for today had been quite good, and as most of the day's walking was on roads, we had opted to wear trainers, as walking in boots on tarmac was not a good idea. This was our first day's walking in trainers, and we were looking forward to it. With our lightweight footwear making our walking easier, Neil almost forgot to whinge at me about the hills, and we strode north-eastwards not quite touching the south-eastern corner of the moor. The scenery was lovely to our left, looking out onto the vast expanse of moorland, some densely wooded with conifers, other parts rocky and inhospitable, and some good looking grazing land for the sheep and cattle which wandered aimlessly around the valleys and hills. On seemingly unused roads now, we made good time to South Brent, passing through some beautiful villages and hamlets. Continuing to head north-east, we were always fairly close to the A 38, although we never noticed it. The main thing we noticed about that morning was how quiet it was, and although we knew it was Sunday, it still felt almost eerie.

We reached Buckfastleigh at lunchtime (whatever time that was!) and Phil and Lyn met us for a pub lunch. Although we were happy to be wearing lightweight footwear, it seemed that trainers were not as good as boots as far as blisters were concerned. We were both suffering, only from small blisters, but as you know, these can soon develop into huge pads. We carried out some minor surgery, expelling the water from the offending areas, and covering them with purpose made blister plasters (also referred to as plister blasters depending on degree of sobriety!) which we discovered were absolutely brilliant, before heading off to the north towards Ashburton, passing Buckfast Abbey, where the Monks of a few years ago had made history by becoming the first Monks to be prosecuted by Customs and Excise! The story goes that the Monks of Buckfast Abbey used to make alcoholic beverages (i.e. cider) to sell to the tourist trade and supplement their meagre existence. However, their methods of testing the stuff for its alcoholic content were a bit antiquated, and they got to the stage where they didn't test it very often, and when they sold one batch, labelled as (x)% alcohol, and people started falling over, Customs and Excise discovered that it was actually 3% stronger than advertised, and prosecuted them for evading payment on that extra 3%!! Bloody beaurocrats. They should all be shot!

On reaching Ashburton, a lovely little market town, we veered east, crossing the A 38 and taking the minor roads again up the Dolbeare road, and then followed the road through the beautiful Kestler Brook valley to Longstone Bridge, there turning left to Combe. Then we had to sing for our beer, or so it seemed. What kind of person names two neighbouring villages Higher Herebere and Lower Herebere? I couldn't reach the high notes, and Neil can't sing anyway, so it seemed as if we would just have to walk on through to Newton Abbot! The last three miles or so were all on the main A 383, and although we did see a large bird of prey (probably a buzzard) fly across a field and into some woods, this last bit of the day's walk was not very enjoyable, especially for Neil, who was suffering from badly blistered feet now. Never mind, tonight we're being looked after by Brother Ben, from The Newton Abbot Lodge of the Royal Antediluvian Order of Buffaloes. We were looking forward to that.

Having been in touch with Phil and Lyn by mobile 'phone during the afternoon, we met them, as arranged at Newton Abbot railway station at about half past five, and awaited the arrival of Brother Ben. After about ten minutes we couldn't help noticing the sound of a car being driven at very high revs along the road towards us. A grey-green Volvo saloon turned into the station car park, with steam pouring from every possible orifice, lurched to a halt beside Phil's car, and out from the passenger seat staggered a failed audition from "Last of the Summer Wine"! You've guessed, haven't you? Yes, this was Brother Ben.

Phil and Lyn had spoken to Ben earlier in the day, and it had been arranged that they would stay at Ben's house, while Neil and I would stay with a friend of his. If you have never met the archetypal West-country man, then you have never met Ben Forth. Neil says he looks like a cross between Amos Brearley and Osama Bin Laden! My immediate impression is of a cider drenched yokel who doesn't like to let his brain interrupt his mouth. He fills the gaps between proper words with nonsensical grunts, or just holds the last syllable long enough to reorganise his mouth to cope with the next word, almost as if to prevent anybody else taking part in the same conversation. And all the time he strokes his very full beard, thereby muffling the already indistinct tirade.

As Phil's car is already packed to the gunwales with our gear, Neil decides that I should travel in Ben's car back to his place where we are to shower and change. Fair enough, I'm game for a laugh, and my insurance is pretty reasonable! So I jump in the back, and away we go, Ben's wife (whose name I am ashamed to say I can't remember) carefully selecting a gear, any gear, then making sure that the engine is revving sufficiently that the car will move no matter which gear she has selected, and Ben shouting instructions at her which she totally ignores!!!

The journey to Ben's place was probably only about ten minutes, but it seemed like an hour to me. When we arrived, I scrambled from the back as quickly as I could, just in case Ben's wife should stall the engine in third gear at four thousand revs! I reckon that was how she had accumulated so many dents in the front bumper, and was probably the reason she was wearing a neck brace. Never mind, we got there in one piece, and without losing Phil and Lyn.

We unloaded the cars and, weighed down with rucksacks, sleeping bags, plus our usual day packs, stood in Ben's front garden while he and his wife argued over who had the door key! In the end the argument stopped when the door was opened by a gaunt young man who introduced himself as Trevor, the lodger. We gratefully accepted his invitation inside, where we wondered if this was a good idea after all. There were floorboards missing in the hallway and on the stairs, and the stairs were half blocked by a huge roll of carpet laid lengthways up them! Liberally scattered around the house were large cider bottles, in varying stages of emptiness.

Ben says that he would have loved to feed us, but as we're late (I don't recall arranging any times, and nor does Phil!) we'll have to go out for dinner. He does however offer us the choice of tea or coffee: Neil and I ask for tea, Lyn and Phil plump for coffee, and we sit down for a chat with Trevor. Enter Ben from stage left: "I've run out of tea bags"! Neil and I both reply that we'll take the coffee instead. Ben hovers in the doorway for a couple of seconds before admitting that he has no coffee either! "I've got some cider if you want?"!!!! We politely decline his offer and he sits down to join the conversation with Trevor.

Neil and I find our way upstairs and use what is to be Lyn and Phils' room as a changing room, as it is closest to the bathroom. The bathroom is in the same state of repair as the rest of the house, and it takes me five minutes to work out that the shower only provides hot water if you hold the shower head at knee level! So I enjoyed (!) a largely cold shower, which at least served to wake me up, and went and divulged my news to Neil. After his shower we made our way downstairs to be told to hurry up or we'll be late for the Buffaloes Lodge meeting. Ben and his wife then proceeded to stage a full scale domestic dispute over whether Ben should be driving in his state, and after a few minutes they come to the conclusion that it would be better for all involved if she drove! I managed to engineer a seat for myself in Phil's car, and we set off for Dartmouth, to visit Ye Olde Lodge.

I must have "MUG" tattooed on my forehead! Ben decided that he was coming in Phil's car as well! We set off, following Ben's wife with Neil in their Volvo, and I somehow wished that I could swap places with Neil, as Ben launched into a guided tour of wherever we were going! The conversation was punctuated frequently by coughs, belches, and exclamations as to where the silly cow thought she was going, (whoever the "silly cow" may have been!), and the highlight of the journey for me, was when I pointed out to Lyn a Buzzard gliding along the ridge of a hill. "Buzzard, that ain't no bloody Buzzard, there ain't been no bloody Buzzards in Devon for over fifty years!" informs Ben. I politely inform him that, as a fairly keen ornithologist myself, I believe that he may be mistaken, and am instantly ridiculed as a foreigner who knows nothing but thinks he knows it all. "I've been a member of the R.N.I.B. for thirty years!" Ben shouts, "I should know what I'm looking at!". Well, I should think The Royal National Institute for the Blind would encourage hobbies, but I feel that ornithology is probably a little awkward for the visually impaired!!! I nearly wet myself.

The journey took a lot longer than I had expected, but then as a foreigner, I couldn't be expected to know how long it should take, could I?! When we eventually arrived in Dartmouth, Ben decides that we're too late to eat before the Lodge meeting, so we'll have to wait until about ten for our food. As politely as I could, I told him that we were not prepared to wait that long, as we hadn't eaten since lunchtime, and we needed to replenish our systems NOW. So Lyn, Phil, Neil and I wander off in search of a curry, chuckling as we related the tales of the journey down to Neil, who I am sure almost wished he had been with us!

We exited the Royal British Legion club where the Buffs' Lodge meeting was taking place, and could smell curry as soon as we got out of the building. So we walked down to the Harbourside, a beautiful area of Dartmouth, but distinctly lacking in food outlets, then turned left up a sidestreet, all the while sniffing the air and assuring each other that we couldn't be far away, as we could all smell curry! We asked people, we spread out in different directions, we tried everything to find the source of the smell, which by now had us salivating, and almost desperate! Then, at long last, we found it. Right next to the British Legion club where we had started!!! When we stopped laughing we went in, and had one of the best bought curries I've ever had. (Nothing will ever compare to Mum's curries!) It took us about an hour and a quarter to finish our meal, and we made our way to the Buffs meeting feeling much better, and ready for a couple of beers.

As we arrived in the bar at the British Legion Hall which houses the Buffaloes Lodge, the atmosphere became somewhat icy. We had obviously been expected to grab a quick fish and chips and return to the Lodge as quickly as possible. Ben's wife was of the opinion that it was not worth our while visiting the Lodge now, as they were nearly finished, but we insisted that we should, so after a short discussion we were pointed in the right direction.

We knocked at the Lodge door and awaited a reply, which was a little while coming, and upon our arrival we made our official introductions and took our seats. There were about fifteen members of Ye Olde Lodge present, and they ranged from the sublime to the absolutely ridiculous! The Worthy Primo looked as if he had just come off a street in a Dickens novel, and between slurps of cider, he mumbled at his Lodge, occasionally receiving a mumbled reply. He was hardly sober enough to talk coherently let alone run a Lodge! Brother Ben was actually one of the more civilized people there! We got talking to one of the brethren who sat at the back with us, and he turned a sympathetic ear to our predicament, understanding our need to eat a proper meal before drinking with them. He made a brief explanation to the Lodge, who all seemed to accept that maybe they had been a little hasty in their judgement of us, and I made a short speech thanking them for their hospitality, which seemed to go down very well. So all was well after all!

At Lodge closing time, about ten o'clock, the Lodge invited all the ladies up to their meeting room, and proceeded to unveil the surprise of the night. They had prepared a veritable banquet for us, buffet style, but humungous all the same. There were pies and pasties, sandwiches and rolls, vol-au-vents, pickles, cheese and biscuits, seemingly never ending plates of sausage rolls, and a few cakes to finish off with. Obviously this was a bit of a challenge so soon after consuming a large curry, but we did our best, and it did explain why they had been so miffed at our apparent indifference to their offer of "food later", which, had it been made clear what had been prepared, may have made a difference to our choice of cuisine for the evening!

After half an hour or so of answering questions about our walk so far, and detailing our route onwards, we persuaded Brother Ben that it was time to leave, and said our farewells to the Lodge. The journey back to Newton Abbot was less eventful than the journey down had been, as Ben was now asleep! We woke him as we reached the town, and he directed us to the home of his friend, Bill, (Bill and Ben eh? I wonder if that was fate?!!) who greeted us and showed us the facilities, which consisted of a single bed and a sofa, and a coin to toss to see who got what! Neil got the bed, so I was on the sofa. Not the most comfortable night's sleep I've ever had but what the heck, I was just glad that we were at last in a civilized dwelling! Bill was a decent bloke, making us a cup of tea before bedtime, and leaving us to ourselves to chuckle about the evening's experiences before Neil made his way to bed.

Monday 20th May. Awoke at seven in the morning, tea already made for us, and Bill ready to take us to Ben's house to meet up with Lyn and Phil. When we arrived there the smell of breakfast was discernible from the road, and Bill came in briefly while we ate our fill, listening to Brother Ben planning his walk from Newton Abbot to Lenham, then we said goodbye to our hosts, and Phil drove us back to where we had finished the day before. I set off on my own, while Phil and Lyn took Neil to find a chemists shop to get something to treat his blisters, and as I walked I was able to put into perspective the "horrors" of the previous night. Ben may be a bit of a piss-artist, even more so than Neil and I, but when all is said and done, he gave up his own bed for Lyn and Phil, and organised a resting place for Neil and myself, and that was more than anyone else had done so far. So for all my criticism of him, the fact remains that he would almost certainly do anything for anyone, and for that I applaud him. Ben, if you're ever up our way and need accommodation, give me a shout: I couldn't turn you away!!

I followed the A 380 across the River Teign estuary, then turned right onto the A 381 past Bishopsteignton and into Teignmouth, where I was glad the railway station provided free access to the toilets! That curry was wonderful!! From there I took the Coastal Path heading north-east towards Dawlish. The weather was quite rough, and the spray from the waves was following the southerly wind, and trying to clear the sea wall to get onto the railway line which ran along the bottom of the cliff. Mostly the spray failed in its attempts, and landed on me! About half a mile along the sea wall to Holcombe, I got a very nasty feeling that the path would become impassable around the headland at Holcombe, and I couldn't see a route on the map to get around it, so I started to make my way back to Teignmouth to follow the roads. Then I saw another lunatic walking towards me, rucksack peeping over his shoulder, and walking with a very determined stride, as if he knew exactly where he was heading for. Which as it happened, he did! We teamed up and walked together along the sea wall to Holcombe, then dived through a tunnel under the railway line, and scrambled up a steep slope the other side until we met the B 3199. This was where we parted, as he lived here and I didn't! He had only been to Teignmouth to do his shopping!

I walked about 200 yards along the road, then rejoined the South West Coastal Path and followed it to Dawlish where Neil rejoined me, having repaired his blistered feet. Together we walked through Dawlish, and on to Dawlish Warren where we met Phil and Lyn for a pub lunch. After lunch Phil decided that he would join us for the short walk to Starcross, from where we would catch the ferry to Exmouth. We soon discovered why Phil had chosen to walk this stretch , as it was almost perfectly flat all the way!

I had made a phone call earlier in the day to Garth Gibson, the Town Crier of Exmouth, who had agreed to meet us at the ferry dock in Exmouth, and direct us to the Beacon Hotel, where he had arranged accommodation for us for the night. I called him again from Starcross, and he was still on course to meet us, so we wouldn't need the map from here onwards for the rest of the day! The Starcross ferry was the biggest we'd been on so far, looking more like a pleasure cruiser than the little ferries we had almost got used to, and as we set off down the River Exe, we had perfect views of the nature reserve at Dawlish Warren, with all manner of birdlife wading along the mudflats and swooping across the vast expanse of wet sand.

We docked in Exmouth at half past three and Garth met us, true to his word, fully robed in magnificent green and gold, and looking very splendid. He walked with us to The Beacon Hotel, which was very comfortable indeed, and then we made arrangements to meet later at the Museum, for a ceremony to open the new wing. Phil and Lyn arrived eventually, having got lost en route, and we unloaded our gear and said goodbye to them, as this was the last stage of their support.

Neil and I were feeling fairly fresh, as today's walk had been short and mostly pretty easy going, and we showered and changed, me into my Town Criers outfit, and we went out - - - - - - - - - - well, as far as the front door, to discover that it was now chucking it down with rain. So we did what we always did in this situation, and went to the bar. I think Exmouth is probably the furthest West I've drunk Shepherd Neames' Spitfire Ale, and very nice it was too! We introduced ourselves to a few of the Beacon Hotel's residents, and when the rain started to ease off, we left. Only to the pub next door though, because as soon as we got out of the door the rain came down even harder than before. At about twenty past six the rain had eased off enough for us to make a dash for it down to the town centre, only about half a mile away, to find the Museum, and meet Garth again.

The Museum at Exmouth is housed in a terrace of old houses, or so it seemed to me. There is a complete history of Exmouth in maybe five rooms, and we were fascinated by it. Not normally being the sort of people to visit Museums, Neil and I enjoyed the experience tremendously, and I would recommend anybody who is visiting Exmouth to pay their Museum a visit. We were introduced to the Mayor of Exmouth, and had our photograph taken with the Mayor and Garth and a couple of other local dignitaries, before Garth took us to the Powder Monkey, a Wetherspoons pub in the town, where we partook of some ale, some very reasonable food, and had quite an amusing conversation with several members of the Devon Cricket Team. Now I know that they only play minor league stuff, but you should see the size of these guys. The smallest of them, the wicket keeper, is about my size, i.e. six feet plus, and built like a prop-forward!! I spoke to one of them about arranging a tour for Lenham Cricket Club, but I think I'll leave it until after I retire from playing the game!

We left the Powder Monkey at half past nine, and had a couple of pints in the Beacon Vaults (the pub next to the Beacon Hotel) on the way back, eventually getting to bed at half past eleven, suffering from the occasional fit of the giggles when we remembered where we had been last night.

We were sad to think that Phil and Lyn were not going to be part of the walk anymore, as they had been brilliant company, and very supportive. They had been there whenever we had needed, and sometimes when we had not. It had been a great four days.

Chapter 4

EXMOUTH TO WIMBORNE MINSTER

Tuesday 21st May. After a good night's sleep, we were up at seven, full of the joys of spring, looking forward to a day which would bring around a first for us: Our fifth consecutive day on the road. A quick wash and brush up later and I was on my way to the launderette to get some smalls un-smelly! We had spotted the launderette the previous evening, and it was only about 300 yards from the hotel, so we decided to start the wash before breakfast thereby saving valuable time. I loaded the machine, bought a small packet of washing powder from the machine on the wall and emptied it into the correct drawer, put my money in the correct slot, and switched on. As soon as the machine leapt into action I was off up the road to the hotel for breakfast.

Just as we finished breakfast our new support crew, John and Michelle Barrett arrived, and we loaded their car with our gear (minus a few smalls!) and arranged with them where to look for overnight accommodation, which we had decided would be around Branscombe. They offered to wait for our smalls and take them as well, but we didn't want to delay them as they were combining their duties as support crew with a family holiday with their two young children, and anyway, we could manage to carry a few pairs of pants with us, I'm sure!

A short while later we returned to the launderette to find all our smalls still smelly! The machine wasn't working. Oh sh*t! What a waste of time and effort. What a good job we hadn't agreed to let John and Michelle wait for our laundry!! We transferred our washing to a machine that worked, paid for more washing powder, set it going, and disappeared into town to waste an hour or so. We were wandering around Exmouth looking for a newsagents when a voice called out to me and I turned to find a lady who looked vaguely familiar. It turned out that she is the sister of a friend of mine, Jim Constable, and I had been chatting to her in The Red Lion in Lenham no more than a month ago! I had mentioned to her that we would be walking through Exmouth, and as she lives there, she had said (jokingly) that she would keep an eye out for us! After a brief chat we excused ourselves and made our way back to check on the laundry. We did manage to purchase some more blister plasters and some antiseptic cream, so all was not wasted, but it was still going to cost us an hour and a half of our walking time. Not impressed!

Once we had got back to the hotel and collected our day packs (including spare pants!), we eventually set off along the Coastal Path at 1015. The going was fairly good for the first three miles or so until we reached the Devon Cliffs Holiday Park on the coast near Straight Point. Two points to make here: Firstly, surely if a point is not straight it is no longer a point?!, and secondly, it was interesting to see that the holiday park is right next to a M.O.D. Firing range. Now I would hazard a guess that when the rookie soldiers are trained on this firing range, their rifles should point out to sea, but what a place to have hundreds of squealing brats doing their utmost to annoy their parents? I can just imagine the conversation: "That's it, nobody loves me, I'm going to run away!". "Okay, son, if you just hop over that fence and head south, that's the best way to go!" . . . . BANG!

As we passed the holiday park, the path became steep and difficult to walk on, with little outcrops of rock here and there, slippery clay and stone under foot, and when we had to climb through a fence to avoid where the coast path had fallen away, there was long grass to wade through. As we struggled along the top of the cliffs towards Budleigh Salterton we became a bit downhearted. When was it going to become easier? I don't really know what we had expected, but it seemed that all the forces of nature were conspiring against us: The hills all had dodgy surfaces, even when dry, the rain always seemed to blow into our faces, even when the wind was behind us, and the roads we took when the footpaths became too tough going were narrow and busy.

At this point we were glad it was dry, although for how long, we weren't sure. The wind was howling across the clifftops, fortunately from directly behind us, but it made the scenery look very wild and not at all welcoming. The sky was full of dark and threatening clouds, which raced along ahead of us leaving us feeling as though we were making no headway at all. We trudged down into Budleigh Salterton feeling very low.

We stopped at a little bakery in the main street to cheer ourselves up with a sausage roll and a sticky cake, and looked at the map to discover that the route from there on for the next four miles was low lying and flat(ish). So we continued our walk with a little less trepidation, along the seafront to the furthest eastern reaches of the town, where we turned left, heading inland for a short distance following the River Otter to Otterton. Walking through this valley restored our faith in our own route planning, as it was just the break we needed from the stress and strain of the Coast Path. We walked beside the river feeling much happier, but all the while knowing that it was only a temporary respite, as within five miles we would be back on the Coast Path, and it looked pretty rough either side of Sidmouth. However, we were determined to enjoy as much as we could, so we took it slowly along the Otter valley, prolonging the easy part as long as we could!

We reached Otterton and turned right, heading east again to rejoin the Coast Path at Ladram Bay, about two miles west of Sidmouth, then had to climb the cliffs again through the aptly named area of Windgate, before negotiating the tortuous flint and clay slopes down to the town. As we entered Sidmouth all we could think about was a cup of tea, some food, and leave the thoughts of the walk for a while. We found a cafe on the seafront and went in, depositing our boots, waterproofs, maps and bootsocks in the entry porch. The lady at the counter took pity on us and brought us our teas, quiche and more sticky cakes, to our table. Whether she really felt sorry for us, or just didn't want us wandering round her cafe in our soggy socks, I don't know, but we welcomed the gesture anyway!

As Neil and I discussed the remainder of the day's walk, a chap came in and went straight to the counter, obviously on first name terms with the staff, and after a quick muffled conversation with the lady we assumed was the proprietress he came over to us and told us not to use the Coast Path to the east of Sidmouth, as there were reports of 100 mile per hour winds approaching, and the path wouldn't be safe. This enabled us to come to a very quick decision as to the route for the rest of the day: We were going to divert inland. After a short consultation with the map we decided to head north to the centre of Sidmouth then turn right, climbing the side of the Sid Valley, up Salcombe Hill to Salcombe Regis and from there across to Branscombe. We knew that the valley side was fairly steep, but when we reached the foot of the hill, we nearly gave up. We were looking from about ten metres above sea level to a peak of 167 metres! It looked horrendous, and it proved to be just so!

The best thing about that hill was that if we walked backwards it looked as if we were going down it! We had numerous stops for breath, water, and eventually, when we were near enough to the top to not care anymore, a cigarette! I have no doubt that if we could have seen it, the view would have been tremendous from there, but the rain was now going sideways from right to left, and we couldn't see a thing. This was the first time we experienced the "One foot in front of the other syndrome", as we came to call it. When you get to the stage that you don't feel anything anymore, you just keep going like an automaton and don't notice what's going on around you. This can be quite entertaining when a car approaches from the rear. Until the horn is sounded you are totally oblivious to the danger, and we had to keep talking to each other as if trying to keep each other awake!

We were by now seriously doubting whether we could complete our projected day's distance, and it was all we could do to suppress the urge to go into the first pub we came to and get seriously drunk. But when we came to it the pub was shut anyway, so it didn't come to that! John had phoned us earlier and told us that our gear was at The Anchor Inn at Beer (or should that be "our beer was at the Anchor Inn at Gear"?), so we were going to have to walk further than Branscombe anyway, by a couple of miles.

We kept encouraging each other by saying stupid things like "Not far now" when we both knew we were lying, but as we came down into Branscombe, the rain eased, then stopped, and we could see the beautiful surroundings, the deep valley dotted with stone cottages, herds of cattle which must have had two legs shorter than the other two to be able to stand upright on those slopes! Branscombe is a lovely village, although maybe a bit isolated, and we were glad that the weather had lifted for us to appreciate it. As I said, the pub was shut, so we carried on, arriving in Beer at quarter to seven. We had covered about twenty six miles in less than eight hours actual walking time, over some of the roughest terrain, and through some of the roughest weather we had so far encountered. That was damn good going!

As John had left our stuff at The Anchor Inn, and he was coming back the following morning to collect it and take it to our next destination, we thought we had better stay there. So we checked in and negotiated a slightly reduced rate for the night, and took our mound of belongings to our room, performed the usual ablutions, and returned downstairs to the bar. As we sat at the bar feeling very pleased with ourselves for managing to complete the day's distance, we noticed a handpump with a pumpclip advertising Otter bitter, from the Ottery St. Mary Brewery. So we ordered a pint each, knowing that this was a lovely beer, and savoured the beautifully smooth flavour as it caressed our throats and soothed our thirsty bellies. How's that for waxing lyrical on a favourite subject? We ordered our meals, and another pint each, and decided that if this was the reward, we'd quite happily do the same distance in the same conditions tomorrow! After about the sixth pint we decided that if this was the reward, we'd quite happily double the distance tomorrow!!

We lay in our beds that night listening to the sound of waves careering in from the Atlantic and hurling themselves up the slipway in the tiny harbour over which our room looked, as if in an attempt to get to us, and teach us not to try defying the powers of nature again! But the walls held strong, and we felt warm and snug, then it went very quiet and dark for about seven hours!

Wednesday 22nd May. At a quarter to eight on the Wednesday morning Neil announced his awakening with a thunderous fart, and proudly told me that the beer had done its job! Ten minutes later when I plucked up the courage to uncover my nose, I got out of bed and looked out of the window to see another rough looking day, with those Atlantic swells still racing towards the coast and turning into huge waves before crashing up the beach and slipway of the harbour. It was quite a spectacular sight, and one that will stay in my memory for a long time to come.

We were dressed and awaiting breakfast when John arrived to collect our stuff, and we loaded it into his car and asked him to arrange accommodation in Bridport or West Bay for that night, thanking him and wishing him a pleasant day, almost wishing that he would offer us a lift to our overnight destination to avoid the effort and the awful weather!

However, he obviously thought we were made of sterner stuff than that, and we knew at the back of our minds that we couldn't have lived with our consciences had we cheated. We returned to the dining room at the Anchor, consumed a hearty breakfast, and loaded ourselves up for the day.

Before starting the day's walk, we took a wander up into Beer village centre to find a shop that could sell us a film for Neil's camera. Beer is not only a wonderful drink, it is also one of the most beautiful and characteristic places I have ever visited. If you've never been there, and you like virtually unspoilt Devonshire fishing villages, then it's worth going out of your way to find, although I get the feeling it may get busy during the height of the holiday season. We found a shop to sell us a film, and I bought a waterproof disposable camera at the same time, so now we could take photos of the rain!

We set off along the Coast Path at half past nine, almost immediately meeting one of the locals who we had met last night in the bar. He was going to the pub, as he did every day at this time, and we marvelled at the way of life here: This guy had been going to the pub twice every day for the last twenty years since he retired!! He wished us luck and we carried on, finding the going a bit dodgy in places, but it was only a mile or so to Seaton where the seafront was a welcome length of flatness before we crossed the River Axe and ascended once more on the South West Coast Path, through a golf course where the path kept disappearing into bunkers or well manicured greens, and up onto the cliffs again. As we searched for the path across the golf course yet again, I stopped and Neil walked into my back before realising that I had spotted a vixen, trotting along directly towards us and, remarkably, downwind from us. She came closer and closer until she was about twenty feet from us, and just as she laid down in the long grass, she must have caught a whiff of human sweat or one of Neil's farts, as she sprang to her feet and disappeared like a Ferrari into the nearest copse. We both started breathing again, and agreed that that was the closest we had ever been to a fox in the wild.

As we neared the end of the golf course, we noticed a section of what I believe golfers refer to as "light rough" at the edge of the fairway, which had dropped dramatically, about three feet, right at the edge of the cliff. I would have had to have been playing for a Hell of a lot of money, and damn sure of winning, before you would have got me to retrieve a ball from there!

The rest of the morning's walk was through some of the most glorious coastal countryside I have ever had the pleasure to walk through. Yes, it was tremendously hard work clambering up 45 degree slopes covered with moss and lichen, along crumbly sand paths, over fallen tree boughs, constantly rising and falling between sea level and about 100 metres (the highest point that morning was nearly 150 metres), but we had now forgotten the stresses and strains of yesterday, and were almost bouncing along! Our route took us along clifftops and narrow ledges, through densely wooded areas, meadow land and cliffs dotted with sparse vegetation. Over Dowlands cliffs, around Charton Bay, Whitlands cliff, Pinhay Bay, Ware cliffs then down into Lyme Regis.

On our way through Lyme Regis we stopped and bought ourselves an ice cream each, and walked along the front like a pair of naughty schoolboys! Unfortunately the tide was in, and the sea was still rough, so we were forced to keep to the South West Coast Path which deviates slightly inland, instead of taking the alternative beach path along the bottom of The Spittles, Canary Ledges and Black Ven into Charmouth. The most unfortunate part about it was that the Coast Path climbs to about 170 metres in the two miles between Lyme Regis and Charmouth, so we had some serious climbing to do. But then we would have missed all that scenery if we had been at the bottom of the cliffs!

Charmouth is a heavily commercialised seaside town, and we had no problems finding a place to get some lunch, and although the quality was a bit less than we had been used to, it was perfectly adequate. After lunch we went to the tiny harbour area, which is actually just the mouth of the River Char, and watched the giant waves pounding the coast. We took some photos before heading east once again, this time going slightly inland to walk along the A 35. The morning's walk had been lovely, but had really taken its toll on our feet and legs, and we had decided once again that an easier walk was necessary for the afternoon. That idea didn't last long! We soon got fed up with the lorries and buses whipping past us with inches to spare, and after about five miles we turned right onto a tiny lane which ran through a valley then back over the A 35 and into the southern edge of Bridport. We stopped at the Leisure Centre and called a taxi to come and take us to West Bay, where

John had arranged our overnight accommodation, as this was slightly off our route, and we didn't think it would be cheating!

We arrived at our B.&.B. at six o'clock, and were made very welcome by the landlady, who brought cups of tea to our room, and offered to give us a discount on the usual rate as we were doing such a good job for charity. We gratefully accepted both the tea and the discount, and set about performing repairs to our seriously blistered feet. Boots off, socks off, blister plasters and several layers of skin off, and we laid on our beds for half an hour to allow the feet to dry out properly. A quick shower, then more drying out time, then dress for the evening, and out to eat.

As we walked into the village centre to find a suitable eating establishment, I was surprised to see the masts on the yachts in the harbour swaying violently, and I thought that a large boat must have been through the harbour to cause such a swell. I had been to West Bay before, and I knew it to be one of the best sheltered harbours on the south coast. But when we rounded the corner and saw the waves rushing straight through the harbour entrance, which acted as a funnel and only served to increase the depth of the waves, we stood and gaped. The waves were surging through with such force that they were smashing against the far side of the harbour wall, and the little pontoon type bridge across the north end of the harbour was being thrown up and down like a Meccano bridge! The power of nature has always amazed me, and this sight only served to heighten that amazement.

We ate a very good meal at The George Inn, partaking of a couple of good beers at the same time, then walked over to the other side of the harbour area to the Bridport Arms Hotel. I had visited the Bridport Arms a couple of years before, and knew it to be a good watering hole, but was shocked when the barman and one of the barmaids recognised me! We had a pleasant evening there, and left at about ten o'clock to make our way back to the B.&.B. where we once again exposed our feet to the air to get them properly dry.

Chatting as we did about the experiences of the day, we both came to the conclusion that despite the physical hardships and the psychological lows that we were occasionally suffering, we were enjoying the walk more than either of us had initially anticipated. It was nice to know that Neil was enjoying it as much as I was.

Thursday 23rd May. Up at seven thirty, bathe the feet, and dress them with blister plasters, then a leisurely breakfast before John arrived to cart our gear to Puddletown where we were heading for today. We said goodbye to our landlady and got on our way at quarter past nine, heading back up to the Leisure Centre before turning right into Bothenhampton and onto footpaths to take us to the village of Shipton Gorge. The weather today was absolutely perfect for us, with a light wind blowing from the south west chasing woollen clouds across the sky, and putting smiles on our faces as we left the noise of the busy A 35 around Bridport, and headed into the rolling hills of the Dorset countryside.

The first eight or nine miles of today's walk were on minor roads and footpaths, before joining the A 35 at Kingston Russell and following it into Dorchester, where we were to meet Alistair Chisholm, the Dorchester Town Crier, and National Champion, before heading out to Puddletown for our overnight stop.

The footpaths to Shipton Gorge were pretty good, and we made it that far without getting lost, then we discovered that a lot of the signed footpaths in Dorset don't actually exist! We found a signpost saying "Footpath to Chilcombe" which pointed directly east across a ploughed field, with no marks to suggest that anybody had ever walked across there before. We followed the compass (because it was in front of us!), adjusting our direction as the map showed a slight deviation in the line of the path, keeping as close as we could to the valleys and so avoiding the steep hills which although affording splendid scenery, looked daunting to have to climb. Then we came to a wooded area which was fenced off and ran at right angles to the footpath, so we walked a couple of hundred yards each way looking for a stile or a gate, and found nothing. So we climbed the fence and scrambled our way through the dense undergrowth to emerge on the eastern side of the copse none the wiser! We studied the map, took bearings with the compass, pinpointed landmarks, and located ourselves! As far as we could make out, we were still on the footpath, so we carried on and got even more lost, and eventually came to a road which wasn't there. We followed the road which wasn't there until we arrived in Litton Cheney, which was there, and stopped to consult the map and try to work out where we had gone wrong. We never did quite work that one out, but never mind, we were back in civilisation now, and only a couple of miles from the A 35 and although we didn't want to leave the scenic footpaths, we also didn't want to keep on getting lost, so the A 35 was quite a welcome stage of the day.

As we marched briskly along one of Dorset's tiny lanes, occasionally greeting a curious cow or a startled sheep, but more often completely alone, we heard a vehicle approaching from behind us, and dropped into single file to allow it to pass. Said vehicle crawled up behind us so slowly that we turned as one to see who was winding us up, and were greeted by a grinning policeman sitting behind the wheel of his big 4 wheel drive wagon. He politely enquired as to what we were doing, and we, equally politely, told him. Satisfied that his enquiries were now complete, he bade us good luck and disappeared into the Dorset countryside. He never did ask us for any form of identification, so I must assume that we're just honest looking!

The incredible scenery we had encountered that morning had been supplemented by the absolute quietness of the slumbering Dorset countryside. I think the loudest sound we had heard that morning had been the barking of a dog from about half a mile away, and other than that the birds and the bees and the breeze in the trees had been our only company. But now we could hear the rumble of heavy traffic, and we knew our route was going to be thundering juggernauts all the way from here.

Two miles along the A 35 we reached Winterbourne Abbas, where we marched into the first pub we came to, which had a sign outside bearing the news that the pub served "good home cooked food", ordered two pints of lime and soda, and asked if we could order some food. Then the bad news. Food is only served until two o'clock. Obviously people in Dorset don't get hungry between two and six in the afternoon. Mind you, the same applies to my local, and numerous other establishments I know, so maybe it's the country that's to blame. I know, let's blame the government, we blame them for everything else! It does seem strange to me that this seems to be the only country in the world that does not cater for people who want to eat at any time other than recognised mealtimes!

We drank our lime and sodas, and munched our way through a couple of packets of peanuts, then got back on the road to try and hit Dorchester as quickly as possible. A reasonable walk of around four miles along the wide verges of the A 35, and we came to the western outskirts of the town, from where I phoned Alistair to ask him where we should meet him. He advised us that the Royal Oak, a Wetherspoons establishment was a good place to meet, and we could move on from there as and when we felt the need, so I accepted his directions, and we got lost again!

After asking directions a few times we found someone who wasn't a tourist, who pointed us the right way, and we met Alistair at about five o'clock. We had already ordered our food by the time he came in, so he watched us eat, and then we moved on, down the High Street to Tom Browns, receiving a detailed tour of the town from Alistair on the way. I'm sure Alistair could have carried on with his informative history of Dorchester for a lot longer than he did, he seemed to know all there was to know about the town, but this was a social evening as much as anything else!

I had asked Alistair if we could visit Tom Browns, as I had been there before and I thought Neil would enjoy it, with its home brewery (The Goldfinch Brewery) at the back, and its rustic charm in the bar. When we arrived Neil's eyes lit up as he spotted the six handpumps on the bar, and I suggested that we should start on the weakest and work our way up, so we ordered three pints of Tom Brown's, and Alistair proposed a toast to our efforts, and wished us good luck and better weather for the remainder of the walk. He then informed us that he would have to leave shortly, as he was catching an early flight the next morning to Boston, Massachusetts, and travelling on to Dorchester, Massachusetts, where he had been invited to speak to the town about the history of the "original Dorchester"! This had come about through the Town Criers competitions he has taken part in, a lot of which I understand he has won!

We listened with interest as Alistair told us a bit more about the history of his beloved Dorchester, and said a grateful farewell when he left, wishing him a pleasant trip to The States and safe journey. Then we set about sampling the rest of the beer. There were only three different ales on sale, so we thought we should try two of each, just to be sure we had got the taste! The Tom Brown's bitter, at 4% a.b.v. was a very full flavoured smooth bitter with a hint of woodsmoke in the finish, the Flashman's Clout was stronger tasting, as you would expect from a 4.5% beer, and was slightly sweeter than the Tom Browns, although not unpleasantly so. Then came the Midnight Blinder at 5%, and the strongest taste of all. I normally think that the stronger beers are too sweet, but my first impression was that it was a very drinkable beer, although probably not a "session beer". Then my tongue became detached from my brain! This seemed to have an adverse effect on my legs, and my eyes tried to follow my feet as they wandered in ever decreasing circles around my boots, which I was still wearing!!! I just about managed to operate the telephone to order a taxi to take us to Zoar House, where John had left our belongings, and we called it a night at eight o'clock.

When we arrived at Zoar house, we were greeted by the landlady, whose top set of false teeth didn't fit, and constantly clattered as she spoke. She was very welcoming, and showed us to our rooms without mentioning that we both stank like breweries, pointing out the dining room, shower, and loo on the way. The house was like something out of The Rocky Horror Show, every floorboard creaking and the doors groaning as they were opened, but at the same time it was very comfortable, and we showered straight away before we settled on our beds to watch a bit of television before our eyes drooped. It was an old fashioned Bang and Olufsen television set, and didn't have a remote control, so Neil was up and down like a yo-yo changing channels until he found something he wanted to watch. Then, after a while, when we wanted to go to sleep, we discovered that we had a problem: There was no off switch! Neil hunted around the entire set, the sides, the back, even underneath! And he still couldn't find it, so I decided that he must be even more drunk than I was, and went over to see if I could find the "OFF" switch. After examining the set closely, the only two buttons with an "O" on them were the "ON" button (which didn't double as an "OFF" button!) and the zero at the bottom of the numbers panel. So I pressed the zero, and hey presto, off she went. Neil was indignant that Bang and Olufsen had the absolute nerve to hide the "OFF" button in that way, and I was in hysterics!!

After some repairs to our sore feet we turned in for an early night, slightly disappointed in ourselves that we had fallen short of our day's mileage target, but comforted by the realisation that we were now well over half way home, and we only had one more day, albeit a long one, until our next day off. And we wouldn't have missed that beer for anything!

Friday 24th May. Woke early this morning, to see good weather, a welcome sight if ever there was one, especially as we had an extra six miles to cover today, due to our lack of willpower in the pub yesterday! We packed all our stuff together ready for John to collect, and made our way downstairs to the dining room for breakfast. Just as our plates of steaming bacon and eggs arrived in front of us, so John turned up to relieve us of our bags, so we formed a quick chain to pass our stuff out to him, and left him to load the car on his own. The landlady made him a cup of tea, and we said our goodbyes, as this was John's last day with us, but we never thought to ask him if we could scrounge a lift back to Dorchester. Never mind, we'd call a taxi, so we asked the landlady if she knew a local taxi firm, and she told us not to bother, she would arrange our lift for us. That was a bonus!

Our lift came in the form of a delivery van which had been delivering groceries to the B.&.B., the driver telling us that he was on his way to Dorchester next anyway, and we weren't taking him out of his way. We sat none too comfortably in the back of his van, ruefully watching the road out of the rear window, thinking that we would be seeing this again very shortly, as this was the road we needed to retrace our steps along to walk back to Puddletown, and then on to Bere Regis and eventually Wimborne Minster. The friendly van driver dropped us right in the middle of town, and wished us luck for the rest of our walk, and we set off, still feeling mildly hungover, heading north-east to Higher Bockhampton, then through Puddletown Forest and into Puddletown.

The route we followed took us along some beautiful lanes and paths, and it was only after looking at the map when we were slightly lost (again) that we saw the course of a Roman Road which we could have followed if we had spotted it earlier! By now we were at the western edge of Puddletown Forest, near Thomas Hardy's birthplace, and we liked the look of the forest, so we carried on. This may have been a mistake, as the footpaths rapidly became almost unusable, due to the huge amount of rain which had fallen over the past 72 hours, and we spent a lot of time picking our way around huge puddles, trying our best not to get our feet wet at this early stage of the day. I know the area is full of places with names such as Puddletown, Tolpuddle, Affpuddle etc., but I didn't realise that they were names of actual puddles!

Once we entered the forest proper we found that we may as well have been on another planet. Mostly coniferous, the wood completely deadened the sound of everything other than the whisper of the wind teasing the upper branches of the trees, and the orchestral birdsong which accompanied us the whole way. And of course, our squelching and cursing as we attempted to negotiate the swamp-like terrain. We came to a small area of dry(ish) grass beneath an ageing sweet chestnut, and stopped there to consult the map and determine the shortest route to a road, any road, as long as it was in vaguely the right direction. As we stood silently poring over the map, we both became aware of a presence close by, and raised our heads slowly to see a small deer about fifty yards from us. The deer obviously knew that we were close by, as it had raised its head and was sniffing at the air. Then, as always happens at the most inopportune moments, I sneezed! I am not one of the fortunate people who have the ability to stifle their sneezes, and the deer must have thought that a scud missile was being launched at it. It took off as if propelled from a catapult, and that brought to an end one of the briefest and yet most memorable moments of the walk so far.

Our studies of the map had concluded, and we headed on, not for the nearest road, the A 35, but for a minor road about a quarter of a mile to our east, at the eastern end of Tolpuddle Hollow. Once we reached this road, at Beacon Corner, we followed it north-east to Puddletown, where we rejoined the A 35 for a couple of miles to Tolpuddle, there taking a few minutes to see The Martyrs Tree, before setting off again on minor roads through Affpuddle, Briants Puddle, Turners Puddle, Muddy Puddle (!), Bloody Muddy Puddle (!!), and on towards Bere Regis, where we stopped for a quick lime and soda in a pub just off the main street. And where it started to rain again!

As we supped our refreshing pints at a very relaxed pace, my mobile phone rang, and John relayed the details of where he had left our overnight bags. I noted the address down , and thanked him for all his help over the last four days, and he wished us both good luck and there was another chapter gone!

We had waited long enough for the rain to stop, and decided that we would just have to brave it, so on went the waterproofs, and out came the sun! It was to be another one of those infuriating days when the weather couldn't make up its mind whether to rain or shine, so we resigned ourselves to having to scramble in and out of our weatherproof gear every five minutes for the rest of the afternoon, and set off up the road towards Bloxworth. Through necessity we took the A 35, walking between Bere Wood and Wareham Forest for the first two miles or so, the alternative route being more footpaths through woodland which we knew would be too wet for our already sodden boots. At the first opportunity we turned left onto a quieter road which took us into Bloxworth where we turned right, heading east again to Whitefield, then Duke's Hill where we were to stop for lunch.

This section of the walk was the first point I had come across which really made me think that we may not manage to complete the walk. I was depressed by the weather, my feet were aching from the constant pounding on tarmac, and because my feet had got wet they were developing blisters at an alarming rate. Neil had become very quiet as well, and it seemed that we had no time to talk to each other, which was a first, as in the past we had been keen to make each other laugh at every possible opportunity. I didn't tell Neil how I was feeling , but he must have sensed that something was getting to me, because as we approached our projected lunchtime stop he started to make little encouraging comments like "Just think, another three hours and we'll be in Wimborne! Then we can have a day off!". Whether he knew it or not I don't know, but he kept me going through that day.

We had lunch in a lovely pub the name of which eludes me now, but if you go looking for it, it's just north-west of the junction of Quarr Hill and Goodwin's Lane, about two miles west of Lytchett Matravers!

After lunch we walked up Goodwin's Lane, then off onto a footpath through Old Park, which was not as wet as we had imagined it might be, and it saved us about two miles compared to the shortest road route! Old Park is just what it says; a mixture of lush meadowland, deciduous woodland, carefully fenced and obviously well maintained, and with an abundance of wildlife to watch and listen to. We saw and heard woodpeckers, a curlew, snipe, rabbits in their thousands it seemed, a fox, and to cap it all, some more deer. I am so glad Neil had been there to get me this far!

After the joys of Old Park, we were once again onto minor roads, taking us into Lytchett Matravers, where we paused briefly for our customary fag break and a bottle of drink from the corner shop, before making our way out of town on the Wimborne Road. Just the sight of the sign saying Wimborne Road made me feel better, and put a bit of spring back in my step, and the rest of the day seemed to pass quickly and relatively painlessly from there on.

Along the Wimborne Road for about a mile, we came to a junction where we went straight across into Rushall Lane. Hang on a minute, I want to stay on the Wimborne Road, it feels better, it sounds as if I'm going in the right direction! Never mind, the map tells us we're still heading in the right direction, so that'll have to do. Rushall Lane is a very nice area, bordered to the north by woodland, and to the south by open fields, with the occasional detached property hiding behind the hedgerow. We saw a greater spotted woodpecker fly up into a large ash tree and within seconds we heard the quickfire sound of him (or her) beating up the defenceless tree as if it was a long term enemy, then we climbed the small hill into Corfe Mullen, knowing that we were now no more than four miles from our destination for the day.

The pressure was off now, we were nearly there and I had to restrain Neil from taking a detour when he spotted a place on the map called Happy Bottom. It would only have taken us half a mile out of our way, and I wondered if we should go and see this wonderfully named place, as neither of us could imagine what a happy bottom looked like, but the pull of Wimborne and the promise of a(nother) well earned pint (or five) kept us on the road to The Pudding and Pie, a welcome boozer in the East Brook area of Wimborne Minster. And boy, did we celebrate when we got there!! It was beginning to feel as though we had already achieved our goal, and I knew this was a dangerous feeling to get, when there were still another eight days walking to do, but we felt that we had earned a rest, and a rest was what we were going to have!

· After about four pints and a bite to eat we called a taxi to take us to our B.&B., and we met our landlord and landlady, lovely people as we were to find out over the next twenty four hours. Righton Lodge was a superb guest house, all facilities were spotlessly clean and the shower was something else! It had settings which ranged from a gentle waterfall tumbling onto your head to a pressure hose which felt like a sandblaster that was enlarging my bald patch! Simon and Bridget, our hosts, ensured that we knew we were in a non smoking establishment, and informed us that they were going out for the evening, so we wandered outside for a smoke, and as we stood on a bridge over the A 31 quietly smoking and chatting about the events of the last few days, my eagle eyes spotted a pub no more than 100 yards from us!

It wasn't much of a pub, but we only wanted a couple of pints and we'd be away to bed. A couple of local lads wanted to know what we were doing invading their domain, so we explained our presence and got talking to them. As bedtime approached we started to make our excuses, but one of them was very persuasive, and twisted our arms right up behind our backs and took us to his local club, The Oakley Community Centre, for another drink! We were determined to make it a quick pint and get back to our beds, but as we stood there talking to a few more local people, the steward of the club came out from behind the bar and called for some quiet, then introduced us! "These two lads over here are half way through a sponsored walk from Lands End to their village in Kent, raising money for charity, so get your hands in your pockets and give them some dosh!". This was followed by one of the barstaff wandering round the entire bar with a pint jug collecting loose change from all and sundry, and after the steward had changed it all into notes, he gave us £45 and two free pints, ensuring that we didn't get the early night we had promised ourselves! As you may have realised by now, Neil and I are soft touches for a beer, but we decided that night that if it helped to raise a bit more money for our chosen charities then we would just have to suffer it!

After that the evening degenerated into a bit of a booze-up, with everybody wanting to buy us drinks, and most of them succeeding! Thank goodness we've got a day off tomorrow to recover from this! We staggered back to our B.&B. at closing time and were asleep before our heads hit the pillows! A fitting end to eight hard days on the road.

Chapter 5

A Day in Wimborne Minster

Saturday 25th May. Our first task of the day was to find another B.& B. The local Tourist Information Office was very helpful, but as Wimborne was holding a re-enactment of the attempted invasion by the Duke of Monmouth today, all their registered guest houses were fully booked. Simon and Bridget called a few of their contacts within the trade, all to no avail, and then suggested that we try Stakley Lodge, a hundred yards down the road on the opposite side. Neil went down there as I phoned, and between us we managed to book a twin room for the night, although we wouldn't be able to get in there until 5 o'clock p.m.. Simon had said that we shouldn't mention where we had stayed the previous night, as the landlord of the Stakley Lodge Guest House had a problem with Simon and Bridget, something to do with the registration of guest houses with the local authority. We couldn't give a monkey's whether they were registered or not as long as they could put a roof over our heads for the night! So we locked all our stuff in the study at Righton Lodge, and got a lift into town with Bridget, our hostess.

As arranged with Chris Brown, the Pamphill and Shapwick Town Crier and Town Mayor's Serjant, (this is the spelling from the official Wimborne Minster guide!) I was fully robed in my Town Crier's outfit, and when Bridget dropped us off outside the launderette to deposit our smellies for a service wash, a few eyebrows were raised. The owner of the launderette enquired as to what we were doing in Wimborne, and after yet another explanation we followed his directions to The Priest's House, which houses the local museum. We introduced ourselves and were given coffee and biscuits by the museum cafeteria staff, at which point I asked if Chris was around, and was told that he would be with us soon, he was just organising the musket brigade! This was going to be fun with a capital F!

It was now almost half past ten, and as I had arranged to meet Chris at ten o'clock I was slightly apprehensive. Perhaps one of the musketeers had accidentally shot him or something. My fears were unfounded, and Chris appeared at just after ten thirty full of apologies and smiles, forever organising his crew and the staff of the museum. Chris is a tiny fellow, having suffered from polio, and I was surprised that he had made it as a Town Crier, as all the other Town Criers I had met were large, imposing people. As we know, appearances can be deceptive, and Chris proved this to be the case as soon as he started to shout!

Chris introduced us to the Mayor, a lovely lady with a very dry sense of humour, and ushered us outside to start the parade. His young assistant vigorously shaking his bell, Chris introduced us to the gathering onlookers as we marched in some semblance of disorder through the streets of Wimborne to the square next to the Minster. He explained to the crowds that the local authority had been unable to grant us a licence to collect funds for our walk in Wimborne today as another charity had already been granted the only available licence. So we wouldn't be collecting money, but if anybody cared to make a donation, the hat would be passed round shortly. And anyone not making a donation would be stood against the wall and shot! Marvellous!

The parade consisted of us two loudmouths, the Lady Mayor, several local councillors, and about eight members of the local re-enactment society, with Neil wandering amongst them trying to get his hands on a musket! After a brief "photo opportunity" outside the Minster, the parade moved on until we reached the Square by the White Hart pub. Here we were treated to a 3 gun salute by the musketeers before Chris suggested that we may like to join him for a pint at the White Hart. We hummed and ha'd for at least three milliseconds before agreeing, and within a minute or two we were ensconced in the bar with all the musketeers, partaking of some wonderful ale from the Ringwood brewery, and making our acquaintance with as many locals as we could.

As I mentioned in chapter 1, the regularity with which we met people who had some kind of connection with Kent was staggering, and of course today was to be no exception. Whilst chatting to a young lady archaeologist from the re-enactment society, we were introduced to her

Part of the three-gun salute in Wimborne Minster.
In the foreground are Chris Brown, (Town Crier and Town Mayor's Serjant of Wimborne Minster) and The Mayor herself!

The Mayor and Musketeers. At the rear on the left are Neil and Gez

friend Martin Cleggett, who immediately asked me if I had been at Maidstone Grammar School in the 1970s. I couldn't deny it, and he proceeded to tell us the history of his surname. Some of you may know of a small hamlet (not a cigar!) between Marden and Paddock Wood, near Collier Street, called Claygate, and the name Cleggett is a bastardisation of the village name. So we now know a man with a village named after his family!

We chatted about school and what we had been doing since, and it turned out that he had made rather more use of his education than I did. Martin had been to university and was now working towards becoming a fully qualified and experienced archaeologist (the musketeering was only a sideline!), travelling far and wide in his quest for a "scoop"! He'll find it one day, I am sure. Neil had been at the Grammar School at the same time as us, but had been two years ahead of me, and three ahead of Martin, so we blamed Neil for the "turd bashing" that we had endured all those years ago, and had another drink! We soon learned that the re-enactment society consisted mainly of archaeologists, with a few historians thrown in, and a couple of nutters who didn't have anything better to do at the time, and they made a very interesting group to converse with, so an entertaining afternoon was had by all.

As we had no licence to collect for our charity in Wimborne, the fundraising effort was somewhat hampered, and we gave up halfway through the afternoon, having raised just over £40. Blimey, the customers in the Oakley Community Centre had raised more than that in ten minutes last night! But never mind, we're still having a good time, and, as during our last day off, we seemed to be consuming rather more than our fair share of beer!

At 4 o'clock we made our way back to the launderette to collect our clean clothes, and were pleasantly surprised when the proprietor wouldn't accept any payment, insisting that we donate the money to our cause if we wanted! From there we decided that we had time for one more pint in The Cricketers Arms before getting a taxi back to Righton Lodge to transfer our belongings to Stakley Lodge. This we did, meeting our new landlord, who seemed a reasonable sort of bloke despite what we had heard! He had told me on the phone earlier that he would be at home between 5 and 6 that afternoon, so we arrived at half past five to be told that we were only just in time! When I questioned this he explained that he had meant he would be home for about fifteen minutes at some point between 5 and 6 o'clock!! How were we supposed to know what he meant if he didn't make himself perfectly clear? No matter, we were there, and he gave us a key and left us to it, telling us not to make too much noise if we were late home. It was like being a teenager again!

We had a short lie down, during which time I phoned my Uncle Peter to tell him where we were as he was our next support crew for a couple of days, then a quick wash and change before heading back to town for an evening of beer, good company and curry. We hadn't had a curry since Dartmouth, and were beginning to experience withdrawal symptoms, so we had decided to put that right, and I knew there was a good Indian restaurant in town from my conversation with Martin earlier in the day. As we arrived in the town centre again, and were just trying to decide which pub to go to, my mobile phone rang, and when I answered it Simon, our previous night's landlord, asked me if he and Bridget could meet us in town and accompany us for a meal. We readily agreed, and arranged to meet in the White Hart in half an hour, giving us just enough time for a pint in the Oddfellows Arms first. The Oddfellows was a pub I had visited before, and was a tiny characteristic old fashioned boozer, squashed between two shops in the centre of the town. If you're ever in Wimborne Minster and fancy a pint, it's a really strange but pleasant place, well worth a visit.

A short walk across town, only about two hundred yards, and we were at the White Hart, where we had been for most of the afternoon, and we received a warm welcome from the staff, especially Cassie, who had taken quite a shine to Neil. However, we were there to meet Bridget and Simon, and in due course they arrived, just in time to buy us a beer as our glasses were empty (what excellent timing!). We stood for a while, chatting as Neil and I are used to doing in pubs, before Bridget suggested that we should sit down at a table in the corner. We tried to buy a round of drinks, but Simon wouldn't hear of it, insisting that he had offered to take us out for a drink, therefore he was buying. This went down well with us and we made sure that Simon regretted his generous offer by the end of the evening! After a couple more pints we made the natural progression to the curry house, and sat patiently awaiting our meal, twiddling our thumbs and making polite conversation, Simon showing a great interest in the route we had taken from

Lands End to Wimborne, and Bridget seemingly taking more interest in Neil!!

I haven't mentioned this so far, but Simon suffered from the same optical malady (although to a lesser extent) that had so unfortunately afflicted my Marilyn Monroe lookalike in Fowey! As I sat opposite him in the restaurant, I noticed that his eyebrows played tag with each other when he was deep in concentration, wiggling and stretching in strange contortions as his eyes looked at me and the lampshade at the same time! Bridget meanwhile was smiling demurely into Neil's eyes, no such offputting affliction to distract him, yet he did seem somehow distracted. Every now and then he would glance furtively at me and wink or grin, as if trying to tell me something. Then the penny dropped. They were not just after a meal with us, they wanted to carry on after the meal, maybe a swift nightcap back at Righton Lodge, then who knows what?!

It became more and more obvious during the course of the meal that Neil was the target for Bridget's attention, and I became nervous that maybe Simon had plans for me!!! He hadn't actually shown any inclination towards me at this point, but my imagination was running riot, I was sweating through nerves, and I decided to feign illness to get me out of this horrific situation. Then Bridget went to the ladies room, and Simon disappeared in the same general direction, so I told Neil of my fears and he told me of his! His only fear however was that we would end up in a foursome! Bridget had been running her stockinged feet up and down his legs all through the meal, and he was looking forward to getting back to Righton Lodge, provided that I would entertain Simon while he got to know Bridget better! I had to tell him, he had two hopes: No hope and Bob Hope! I was getting out of there!!!

The meal finished, we left the restaurant with me hoping that we could go for another drink somewhere, and maybe spike Simon's beer so he would go to sleep, or fall over and do himself an injury which would disable him temporarily. No such luck. Simon immediately offered us a lift home and Bridget wouldn't hear me refuse, so into the car we got, me babbling incoherently about needing to buy some cigarettes, then in the same breath saying how we must have an early night, as we were to be back on the road at eight thirty in the morning. Bridget drove us home via a garage (which was shut, so we still had no cigarettes, and God, how I needed one right now), all the way I could feel Simon's eyes drilling their way through me via the reflection in the mirror under the passenger sun visor. Neil was enjoying this! Bridget had tilted the interior rear view mirror to look into his eyes whenever she felt the need, and he leaned forward frequently to be closer to her, and in my imagination to caress her neck on Simon's blind side! By now I was sure they must be able to see or feel me shaking. Were they playing a deliberate game with me, or did they think I was sweating with anticipation? Either way, they were going to discover just how wrong they were. I was going to put them straight, and leave nothing to chance. I would tell them firmly but diplomatically that they had wasted their efforts on me, that I was sorry if I had given them the impression that I was "up for it", but they had misread the signs, that they were lovely people but I had no feelings for them other than purely platonic ones.

Then we reached Righton Lodge and I clambered out of the car, nervously checking that Simon wasn't close enough to grab me, and said something along the lines of: "Thanks very much for the curry must dash now got to be up early in the morning (gasp for breath) lovely to meet you!" and shot off down the road to Stakley Lodge with Neil being dragged along in my slipstream! We stood outside the B. & B. long enough for me to get my breath back and offer up a prayer to the God of lucky escapes, until we noticed Bridget and Simon still standing outside Righton Lodge, only a hundred yards away. Then we decided it was time to go inside, to the safety of our little room, and with our friendship still intact.

Then came the next problem. Neil put the key in the lock, tried to turn it, and found that the last people to enter the guest house had put the deadlock on the door! Neil immediately suggested that we should go back to Righton Lodge to see if Bridget and Simon could find us a space on the floor, but as the sweat sprang from my brow again, he chuckled and said "Only joking mate!". So, after knocking gently on the door for a couple of minutes in a vain attempt to wake the boss, we ignored the last order given to us by the landlord of the Stakley Lodge, and made as much noise as we could, hammering on the door, shouting through the letter box, and ringing the doorbell all at the same time, until a very irate host appeared at the bottom of the stairs. His attitude changed as he realised that we had been locked out, and he let us in and was gracious enough to apologise for the inconvenience, before offering us a cup of tea before bed. We politely declined his offer and made our way to our room to discuss the events of the evening, and laugh at my unfounded terror of "Simon the Bum Boy"!!

Once again, we had had such a superb day, and we couldn't fault the people we had met. We seemed to be cursed with bad weather whenever we were walking, but blessed with excellent company and superb food and drink wherever we stopped. Was this trying to tell us something? Ho hum, sleep time now, we've got a long way to walk tomorrow!

Our regular half asleep chat that night was punctuated with giggles and sniggers as we tried to fathom out what the eventual outcome of the evening would have been. I reckon that if our hosts from the previous night had been serious about us they would have made their move there and then. Neil reckons that the first night was just a "sussing out" period, and they had waited for the right moment to make their move. I don't really care now as it's all in the past!

Whether this "experience" was a result of too much beer, or an escape from the harsh realities of our walk, or maybe even the culmination of too many good times in a short space of time, I couldn't say; but it was a weird feeling the following morning trying to establish the truth of what exactly had happened and what was purely fantasy. I know that I have in the past been prone to letting my imagination dictate to me, but for both Neil and I to feel the same must be a huge coincidence.

I must stress that the account above of the evening we spent with Simon and Bridget was just how my ale-fuddled brain saw things. Simon and Bridget are lovely people and I am sure that they had no evil intentions towards either of us.

Chapter 6

Wimborne Minster to Winchester

Sunday 26th May. We were up at half past seven, washed and dressed and ready for breakfast, wondering whether our memories of last night were of reality or a dream! Neil convinced me that they were real, and I was quite glad about that, because it would have taken a terribly perverse imagination to dream it! We settled down to an excellent breakfast, and during our conversation with the landlord we must have let slip where we had stayed the night before last. He told us that if we should bump into Bridget and Simon as we were leaving we shouldn't mention where we had stayed, as they had some kind of problem with him, something to do with not being registered with the local authority. Hold on a minute, haven't we heard this before? Oh, yes, Bridget and Simon had said exactly the same about him! Should we say anything, or let them carry on regardless? Let them carry on!!

Uncle Peter turned up at nine o'clock as arranged, and as soon as we had loaded the car with all our bags, we sprinted off up the road to find a shop to sell us some cigarettes! Desperation had set in and fags were top priority at this precise moment, so we made a bee line for the Oakley estate where we had been the other night, and walked round and round the houses until eventually we found a newsagents. Standing outside the shop gratefully inhaling our nicotine laden smoke, we had a look at the map to see which way we should be heading, and were pleased to discover that we were almost on route.

Once the cigarette smoke had made us dizzy, as it does when you have deprived yourself for a longer period of time than usual, we set off at a steady (not fast!) pace heading east to join the Castleman Trailway past Little Canford to Stapehill, there crossing the A 31and heading around the north of West Moors village and onto a dismantled railway track which carried our chosen path around Ashley Heath and then back to the A 31 just west of Ringwood. We joined the Castleman Trailway at Canford School, a private school in glorious grounds right on the banks of the River Stour. The tranquillity was breathtaking for a few seconds until we noticed the background hum of the traffic on the A 31, which was only half a mile away, but the setting was wonderful. We followed the river for a couple of miles to Canford, accompanied by swans, wagtails, mallard ducks, and the occasional flash 'of brilliant colour which indicated a kingfisher, and when we reached the main road we crossed straight over and into Ferndown Forest keeping to the Castleman Trailway all the way, feeling the cushion of the fallen pine needles underfoot, and managing to ignore the very distant hum of the traffic on the main road. The sun was shining for a change, and it became quite hot at times, so we were grateful for the trees which offered us some shade almost all the way along this dead straight, dead flat but pleasant path to the River Avon at Ringwood.

When we reached the outskirts of Ringwood we stopped for lunch at a pub called The Fish Inn, a lovely old pub in beautiful surroundings, right next to the river, where we had a ploughmans and a pint of lime and soda each, then had to spend a while examining a gorgeous B.S.A. Rocket 3 which was parked outside the pub before hitting the trail again, heading north-east now towards the New Forest, looking anxiously at the sky as it shoved its heavy load of cloud along at an alarming rate. We were now following the Avon Valley Path along the beautiful meandering River Avon, with lakes and gravel pits either side, some trying to upset windsurfers and yachtsmen, others challenging those with more patience to find where the big carp were hiding.

As we reached Rockford, where our route took us away from the Avon, the rain started, and we found a sheltered patch under a huge yew tree to have a quick smoke break and then haul our waterproofs on, cursing John Kettley for the weather, and wondering whether it was worth waiting for it to stop. We were glad we didn't decide to wait, because it carried on for the next hour and a half, by which time we were a further five miles up the road. I say "up the road" because although we had planned to do most of the afternoon's walk on footpaths, when we came to the first footpath on the map it was under a foot of water, with small trees and branches being swept along by the current, so once more we came to the conclusion that the road was the better alternative. At least it was only a small road with wide verges, and the scenery was typical of the New Forest, with small undulations rather than hills, and sparsely scattered trees, with the occasional thicker cluster of trees almost constituting a wood, normally sheltering a small group of ponies or cattle. We had to move off the road at one point in Appleslade Bottom to allow passage of a herd of cattle, who obviously had more right to the road than we had. Well, we were wearing boots and they weren't! This was the only traffic jam we had seen all the way from Land's End, and as it was in such a beautiful rural setting on a tiny country lane, it made us chuckle at the irony of it all.

As we tramped on, the rain ceased and a hazy sun peeped out from behind the dark grey blanket of cloud to taunt us. We could almost hear the words; "Go on, take your waterproofs off, then I can really soak you!", and we carried on walking until the clouds had all but disappeared before peeling our sweaty nylon coats and leggings off, once again cursing John Kettley and all the other weather forecasters for their gross incompetence. We stopped several times to take photographs as we negotiated the ponies and their young, some of the foals we saw can only have been hours old, as they were still damp and struggling to stand upright. Mind you, we're more than hours old, and if my memory serves me right it was only about twenty hours ago that I was having trouble standing upright!!!

By now we were crossing Broomy Plain, with only about four miles to go to Fritham, where we would look for a B.& B. before calling Peter to deliver our overnight stuff, and we were feeling O.K. When I had been route planning I had assumed that wherever we went in the New Forest we would be falling over bed and breakfast accommodation, with no need to book in advance, as it was out of season. How wrong could I have been?! As we walked into the village, we passed a couple of likely looking places, but enquiries brought negative responses on both counts, so at about half past five we called Peter and asked him to pick us up and take us back to their place in Ashley, near New Milton. It was a fair distance, but we had no realistic options. So guess what we did? That's right, we went to the pub!

The Royal Oak in Fritham is the only boozer for miles around, and was packed to the brim with yuppy types with their £200 boots and

£300 jackets, who had probably walked a couple of miles to the pub to show off their Cherokee Jeep keys and their Pierre Cardin sunglasses to each other, so we grabbed a couple of pints and went and sat outside, as far from the madding crowd as we could get! Peter turned up at a quarter past six and we gratefully threw our waterproofs in the car and followed them with our bodies. We had started to stiffen up by now, and it was nice to take the weight off our feet.

Forty minutes later we were being pampered by my Auntie Jean, who despite having cooked their Sunday lunch earlier in the day, was insisting that she should cook us something there and then. This time we won, and I assured Jean and Peter that we would rather have a lazy shower and then walk to the nearest pub for a bite to eat. Well we nearly won. Peter insisted on giving us a lift to the Three Bells, where he left us to feed and water ourselves before picking us up again at half past ten, and take us home for the most comfortable night's sleep so far.

Monday 27th May. It's morning, and I ache! Not so much the feet and legs, but all over, and we've got a long way to walk today. We had a huge breakfast courtesy of Jean, who seems to be able to make a gourmet meal out of bacon, eggs, tomatoes and toast, and set off with Peter at about nine o'clock, via the chemists to stock up on blister plasters. The forty five minute journey was extended somewhat when Peter took a wrong turn and we had to go all the way into Ringwood before we could turn round and get back on the right road to Fritham, but we still arrived there by ten fifteen, so all was not lost. Peter bade us farewell at Fritham, as he was just taking our stuff to Winchester and we wouldn't be seeing him again (well, not on the walk anyway!).

We set off in brilliant sunshine, once again marvelling at how much better the sun can make you feel, and headed almost directly due east for the first few miles, passing just south of Bramshaw, then turning to the north-east to head through Furzley, on to Blackhill, then Shootash. The planned route thus far was all on minor roads, then from Shootash almost all the way to Braishfield was to be on footpaths. I expect you can guess where this is leading, can't you? Yes, as we approached Blackhill, John Kettley sent over some more clouds. He must have spotted us smiling and enjoying ourselves! As the rain started, we had a very brief conversation which went something like this. Neil: "Sod walking footpaths in this again!". Me: "We could always detour into Romsey along the A 27." Neil: "Like I said, sod walking footpaths in this again!". Decision made, we took the A 27 into Romsey town centre, found a pub that served food, and had an extended lunch break.

After an hour and a bit the rain had eased off to a light drizzle, so we set off again, initially on the A 3090 towards Ampfield, then after about a mile we turned left onto a minor road to Braishfield. This brought us back onto our planned route which was on roads all the way to Winchester. The weather cleared quite nicely during the afternoon, and we made good progress for the remaining twelve miles or so into Winchester, the route being easy going, and with some pleasant though unspectacular scenery to keep us interested until we got to Standon. At Standon we rejoined the A 3090 and were constantly buzzed by buses, lorries and cars as we made our way along the gutters and verges for the two miles to the outskirts of Winchester.

We were heading for the town centre, as Neil wanted to look up an old friend, and we made our way down the B 3040 through West Hill, past the Cathedral, and onto the ring road where we came across a pub called the Mash Tun. Neil suggested that his mate Mick might be in there, so we had yet another excuse to visit a licensed establishment! (As if we needed an excuse!!) In we went and Neil walked straight to the bar and said to the bloke with his back to us "Hallo mate.". Mick turned round slowly and a look of astonishment appeared on his face. "Hallo Neil, what the bloody Hell are you doing here?". "We're on a sponsored walk from Lands End to Lenham, and I thought as we were passing through Winchester I'd come and find you.". After a short pause Mick replied "I would have been less surprised if you'd said 'I don't know.'!" When we stopped laughing we gratefully accepted Mick's offer of a pint, and became involved in a hilarious conversation which detailed the route we had taken so far, some of the people we had met en route, and how long we anticipated the rest of the journey to take. You may think that the subject matter was far from hilarious, but you obviously haven't met Mick! When he and Neil got together, it was like listening to an amateur Peter Cook and Dudley Moore! They really clicked well and had the whole bar in hysterics within minutes.

Another pint later I went outside to phone Alan Kinge, the Winchester Town Crier, with whom we were lodging for the night, and he offered to come and pick us up, so we made arrangements to meet Mick later, back in the Mash Tun, and dragged ourselves outside just as

Alan turned up. He drove us to his home in the Weeke area just to the north of the town centre, and introduced us to his wife, Barbara, then showed us to our room. Then disaster struck.

As Alan led us upstairs I had a premonition that all was not going to be well somehow, and when we entered our room it became clear why. The house was a cattery with provision made for human habitation! There were cats slinking around here, there and everywhere, depositing their hairs all over the house, and although we are generally animal lovers, neither Neil nor I are great cat lovers, and Neil suffers from asthma, and cannot tolerate cat hair around him. We explained our predicament to our hosts, and Neil phoned Mick to see if he could accommodate him for the night, and fortunately he could. We ate a lovely meal with Alan and Barbara, and then we returned to the Mash Tun to meet Mick for a couple of pints. I left Neil and Mick at about half past nine, as they were reminiscing about old times, and got a taxi back to the Kinge household, where I was immediately made very comfortable, with coffee, biscuits, cake and almost anything I could ask for.

Then Alan asked whether I had taken part in many Town Crying Competitions. I explained that although I had been Lenham's Town Crier for over ten years, I had only recently joined the Ancient and Honourable Guild of Town Criers, and had only then realised how seriously the job was taken. I had never entered a competition, and didn't realise how many different ones there were, it had all just been a bit of fun until we planned the walk! Alan then took it upon himself to educate me! We watched a video tape of the European Town Criers Championships from 1999, and Alan and Barbara pre-empted every section of the film, telling me who was appearing next, and his wife's name, and where they were from, and which competitions he had taken part in in which year, and which he had won, and why he had not won others! Between them I would bet that they know every Town Crier in the country, and their spouses, and their history of taking part in and their success rate in competitions!! Even to the point of knowing who had won the "Best Dressed" category each year!

At eleven o'clock I started to make my excuses to get to bed, but Alan had other ideas, and poured me another cup of coffee before putting another video on of yet more Town Crying competitions! Then my mobile phone rang, and as I answered, I was nearly deafened by a blast of heavy rock music so loud that I couldn't hear who was calling me. (That ruled out my Mum!!). I looked at the display panel on my phone and saw that it was Neil calling from his mobile, so I listened intently for a few minutes, just to run his bill up a bit (That'll teach him to wind me up!) and ended the call, much to Alan's delight. I'm sure he was only trying to help by boring me to sleep, but I just wanted to go to bed, and still he was pointing out the faults in so and so's performance at Newton Abbot in 1996, and Barbara was telling me how to recognise a non authentic outfit by the button placings and the lining stitches, all of which is very interesting but not at eleven thirty at night after a twenty five mile walk!!! After a short viewing of my outfit, and the information that my outfit was not authentic (because I chose a Celtic design for the buttons!), they decided to let me go to bed, with their advice about authentic shoes ringing in my ears.

I think I only sneezed for the first two hours of my night in the cattery, and I was secure in the knowledge that no matter how much I scratched myself, there would be more skin underneath!

Alan and Barbara were two of the nicest people you could ever wish to meet, but they both seem to be obsessed with Town Crying, Alan on the practical side, and Barbara on the costume front. Barbara has made costumes for several Town Criers over the years, and each one has been unique and authentic in its design. Their knowledge of the subject is phenomenal, and if I ever need any serious advice on the finer points of the art I will know where to go, but their banter, although tremendously informative, had exhausted me, and as it was now midnight, and our next support crew were meeting us at eight o'clock in the morning, so I would have to be up by seven, which meant I was going to be short of sleep for the next day's walk. Never mind I told myself, they had been so good to me, and had fed and watered us both, and had accepted Neil's escape with good grace. And despite all my whingeing over the last few paragraphs, I like them, and hope to meet them at competitions in the future.

Chapter 7

Winchester to Tunbridge Wells

Tuesday 28th May. I had no need for an alarm clock this morning. I awoke frequently during the night, sometimes sneezing, sometimes coughing, wheezing, scratching, or rubbing my eyes. Bloody cats! From about six o'clock onwards I was barely dozing, waiting for someone to start moving about, to give me the excuse I needed to get up. Eventually at around five past seven I heard movement and sprang from my torture chamber just in time to hear whichever one was moving go into the bathroom! I'm next in the queue!

Alan cooked a smashing breakfast, and when Pete and Christian turned up at a quarter past eight there was still plenty left, so they had a quick bite and a cup of tea, and after we had said our farewells we set off to meet Neil. I phoned him as we left, and got Mick to direct us to his house, and shortly after we went past his house Neil phoned and told us we'd missed it. He had seen us go past, and was highly amused by it all. Pete questioned how the Hell we were going to find our way back to Kent if I couldn't even find my way out of Winchester, and I had the raging hump!

Just as Pete and Chris dropped me off, and loaded the car with Neil's gear, it began to rain, only gently, but it was rain all the same. Mick lived at the south-eastern corner of Winchester, and we only had to walk about a mile and we were out of the City and onto the South Downs Way. As we marched briskly up through the Highcliffe area of Winchester, we had to find a shop for Neil to purchase some breakfast. He may have been laughing at me last night, but at least I wasn't hungover and hungry now! It was now half past nine, and it was still drizzling, but we were almost immune to the wet now. Or so we thought.

Once Neil had consumed his makeshift breakfast (consisting of a cornish pasty, a bottle of cola and a chocolate bar), we made for the South Downs Way. As we found our chosen path, the rain started with a vengeance, being hurled across from right to left almost horizontal, with the occasional bucketful hitting us straight in the face. We stopped and donned our waterproofs at the edge of a playing field between the Highcliffe estate and the footbridge over the M 3, then pressed on over the motorway, following the South Downs Way due east through the little hamlet of Chilcomb. This was a beautiful valley, with small woods dotted here and there, lush grass providing good grazing for the magnificent cattle that roamed the fields, and some almost mountainous hills (or were they hilarious mountains?) all around us. All the way from the motorway we had been listening to the sound of rifle shots, obviously from a M. O. D. range, but as we reached the bottom of the valley either the shooting stopped or the sound was muted by the rain and wind. We walked along in the lea of a thick hedge in the bottom of the valley for about half a mile, then the shelter ran out and we saw the daunting hill in front of us. We were getting very wet now, the rain driving into our faces, threading its way through the tightest of gaps between nylon and skin, and dripping down our bodies, chilling us to the bone as it mingled with the sweat and soaked our underwear.

We started the climb feeling pretty low, and the higher we got, the colder and more miserable we became, reaching the crest of the hill at a place called Cheesefoot Head. I know this area quite well, and it was such a shame that the weather had closed in, as the scenery is some of the best in Hampshire. We crossed the A 272 here, still on the South Downs Way, which joins the Kings Way and carries on eastwards for a couple of miles before the two paths separate again, and where we took shelter in a Dutch barn to have a smoke and try to warm up a bit. It wouldn't have made any difference how many layers of clothes we had put on that morning, they would all have been drenched by now. Our combat trousers were completely soaked beneath our waterproof leggings, and our boots were filling with water, softening our feet to a dangerous state, and we decided there and then that we would not be able to complete our projected mileage today.

After our second cigarette in the shelter of the barn, we pulled our hoods tight around our faces again, leaving just our eyes and noses clear of the stifling nylon, and made our way out into the elements again, almost immediately feeling the cold as the wind pressed our clothing hard against our already cool skin. The route we had chosen was mainly on high ground, planned to give us better views, but also, obviously, more exposed to the weather than a less elevated path. Still, we consoled ourselves with the thought that the paths on a lower route would have been wetter, and possibly completely flooded, so we had probably chosen the lesser of two evils. Then our path disappeared under a pond. It was a big pond, possibly even a small lake, about eighty yards across, and where the path emerged the other side we noticed the inlet to the pond. The rainwater was pouring down our footpath into this huge puddle, and we were now completely miffed!!!

The nearest alternative path was only about half a mile back along our tracks, but as we had passed it Neil had said how glad he was that we weren't following that one. It went straight across a recently ploughed and harrowed field, and as we climbed the stile to commence the crossing, we knew that within a few yards we would be carrying a few extra pounds in weight due to the mud which would cling to our boots. We were right, and as we reached the bottom of the shallow valley and looked up to the farthest point we could see we realised that it was a bit steeper than we had first thought. I started singing to try to regain some rhythm to our legs, and Neil soon joined in which was just as well because I only knew the first verse of "Always look on the bright side of life" from Monty Python's "The Life of Brian"! We muddled our way through about three verses before running out of words altogether, but it put a smile back on our rain sodden faces for a while! We clambered through a fence into a narrow strip of woodland, sheltered while we partook of yet more nicotine, then clambered through the fence on the other side of the copse to find no marked footpath in sight. However there was a sign of civilisation in the form of a house about a quarter of a mile east of us, which at least was in the right direction, so we headed for that. When we arrived at the house it was derelict, and we were sorely tempted to find a dry patch in there and doss down until the rain stopped, but having already made the decision to call a halt at Cheriton, only a mile and a bit further on, we soldiered on through the mud until we came to a road which led straight into the village.

We entered the village at 12:45 feeling like a pair of the proverbial drowned rats, and probably looking much the same, spoke to a lady who looked quite horrified at the state of us, and walked round the corner to The Flowerpots Inn, a place I have been to before. We took our chances there and stripped off in the rear lobby, waterproofs, t-shirts, combat trousers, and socks followed our boots onto the brick floor, then we nipped into the toilet wearing just our underpants to try to dry ourselves off, failing miserably as the only towels in there were paper ones! We wrung our t-shirts and combats out as best we could, re-dressed and made our way to the bar for some liquid sustenance and sympathy. The former was available at a price, but sympathy had been replaced by mirth for the day, it seemed. The barman thought it was hilarious, two nutters out walking in this weather, and it wasn't until one of the kitchen staff came through with food for some other customers, and recognised me, that we got any sympathy at all!

Pete and Chris had answered our S.O.S. call from the Dutch barn, and met us at The Flowerpots at one fifteen with clean dry clothes for us to change into. Some of you may think that with dry clothes and a good lunch inside us we should have carried on walking, but our feet had become so soft in the water that it would have been crippling to continue. So we had a couple of pints of beer from the brewery at the other side of the car park, I was drinking "Cheriton Best", and Neil and the others had "Pots" ale, brewed on the premises, and a wonderful drink it was too! Chris had drawn the short straw and could only have one as he was driving, and having eaten a very good meal and said hello to the rest of the staff who recognised me, we left at half past two, walking out of the pub into bright sunlight, and went straight to the pub where Pete and Chris had booked us in for the night.

The Cricketers Arms is an imposing looking pub with a large car park, just north of the little village of Steep, to the north of Petersfield, and once we were shown to our rooms we knew it would be a comfortable stay. The rooms were huge, and the windows looked out into the welcoming arms of a gigantic horse-chestnut tree, the soothing sound of the breeze teasing the leaves just about audible in the spring air. Neil and I made ourselves comfortable and laid out our wet clothing on the radiators (as instructed by the landlord, who had also taken our boots to the boiler room to dry them out, bless him!), and sat down with the next two day's maps to try and formulate an escape from the mess we were now in! We had fallen about twelve miles short of our mileage target for the day, and now we were so close to home, we didn't have much time to make the distance up. We decided to give it our best shot tomorrow, see how the feet held up, and see how much we could regain. Then we went to find Chris and Pete for a beer!

When we learnt that the bar was closed at three o'clock, and it was now half past, we agreed to share the cost of a taxi to Petersfield and find a pub there! Then the landlord offered us a lift to the town, and our afternoon was sorted. We were dropped in the middle of Petersfield, a town I had driven through before, but knew very little about. My impression had been of a pleasant, sleepy little market town, with a picturesque square surrounded by shops and pubs, and I had always anticipated that the majority of the population would be middle aged or older, almost a retirement town. The first pub we went into had "World Cup 2002" posters all over the walls both inside and out, three big screen televisions set up in the bar, around 90 decibels of modern "pop" music blaring out, and no real ales, while the barstaff were more intent on watching "Neighbours" on one of the big screens than serving beer. Needless to say, we left them to their sad existence and wandered round the square until we found another pub.

This one was more like it! A little street corner boozer, spit and sawdust (without the sawdust!) and loads of character, and a hand pump proclaiming "Ringwood Best". So we made ourselves comfortable, and started to return the banter from the locals, landlady and all. Our expedition had not been publicised on local radio or T.V. around here, so we made the most of what seemed an interested little crowd, and one of them promised to call the local radio station in the morning to get them to announce our presence in the area. What a nice gesture! We were just in the process of filling him in with the finer details of the charities, when Neil nearly fell over laughing. An old boy had just walked in and told his mate a joke, and Neil had been earwigging: Quasimodo walked into a bar and said to the barman "Gimme a whisky!" The barman replied "Bells O.K?" Quasimodo said "Mind your own business and pour my drink!" Boom boom!! Well, we all thought it was funny.

After a few more beers and a marvellous joke session with the locals we left, walking towards the railway station until we found a taxi rank, and getting into a rank taxi which took us back to our B.& B. in Steep, where we arrived at a quarter past seven. We had another beer or two,

Gales "Butser" bitter, with a lovely meal, and went up to bed to give our feet some serious drying time. Lying on our beds with the windows open listening to the hushing of the chestnut leaves and the last few distant notes of the dusk chorus, it was difficult to remember the foul weather that had so spoiled what should have been a lovely day's walk. Neil's feet were the best reminder! The skin across the whole of the soles of both his feet was detached from the next layer, and the cushion of water between the layers meant that when he put his foot to the floor, it seemed as though it was sliding a fraction of an inch before finding its grip!!! I sincerely hope he doesn't suffer too much tomorrow.

Wednesday 29th May. When we awoke this morning, at six o'clock as arranged, Neil was keen to get dressed and on our way as quickly as possible. This was unusual for him, as his laid back attitude normally had me attempting (usually unsuccessfully!) to hurry him along. I thought no more of it, and we packed all our gear away and left it in a tidy heap on the bedroom floor and skipped down the stairs to breakfast. A small breakfast and two coffees later we trotted back upstairs, woke Chris, who was to run us back to Cheriton, and collected our pile of gear to load into the car. Chris was ready in a couple of minutes, and we left our room just as the landlord's assistant came to play chambermaids. Neil was like a man possessed, and we jumped into the car and shot out of the car park before he told us why the hurry.

He was almost crying with laughter as he explained the hurry: You may remember that yesterday morning he had purchased some chocolate as we walked out of Winchester. I hope that you also recall that the weather had been atrocious all morning, and we had got drenched to the skin. The weather had been too bad for Neil to think about eating his chocolate bar, so he had saved it until last night, and attempted to eat it in bed. In fact he succeeded in eating all but a smidgin of it, but that smidgin had found its way into his bedclothes and materialized as a huge "skid mark" on the sheet! What a plonker!

Chris dropped us at the Flowerpots at seven forty five, and we set off in bright sunshine, straight along the A 272 towards Petersfield. We had come to the conclusion that the road was going to be the best option for us until the weather showed signs of improving for longer than a couple of hours, and although the enjoyment factor was going to be reduced, we felt that it was the only sensible option.

We were conscious that we shouldn't walk too fast, as tarmac is completely unyielding to feet, and in spite of the fact that we had somewhere around twelve to fifteen miles to make up as quickly as possible, it would be preferable to arrive late in Lenham on foot, than early on a bus! The A 272 is a lovely road to drive along, and we both knew it fairly well, but we could never have imagined how difficult it would be to walk along. There were stretches without footpaths that seemed to go on for mile after mile, and the traffic that came hurtling down the road towards us seemed to have total disregard for pedestrians, so we frequently found ourselves diving for cover in the verges, or squeezing into hedges full of thorns.

Through Bramdean and on past the West Meon Hut, we got just the other side of Lower Bordean before the weather showed signs of turning nasty. At first we thought we might stop for a while and let the rain blow over, as the forecast we had seen had said "sharp showers", but as it hadn't actually started raining yet we decided to carry on until it did! (Just as well really, as we covered another ten miles before it did!). We reached Petersfield at half past ten, and had a snack at a roadside "burger-bar", washed it down with a cuppa, and set off again before the break made us seize up.

We passed to the north of the town centre and took the B 2070 for a mile and a half towards Liss and Rake crossing the county boundary into Sussex about two miles north-east of Petersfield, before turning right onto some minor roads which ran parallel to the A 272 for a few miles. The immediate relief we felt just to be off the A 272, with its thundering juggernauts and grimy puddle-strewn gutters, was indescribable, and once more we felt happy in our task. The minor roads took us through the beautiful West Sussex countryside with its glorious woodlands and palatial estates as far as Trotton, where we stopped for lunch. Or rather for a rain break. We had planned to have lunch in Midhurst, ambitious though that was, as that would have meant walking about twenty miles in the morning, but we were only three miles short of that target when the rain started. It had actually been spitting with rain for the last mile or two, but at Trotton it began in earnest. The only eatery in Trotton was the pub, and we discovered to our dismay that they were closed for lunch that day due to staff sickness! So we got two bags of nuts and two free pints of lime and soda and sipped them while we waited for the rain to stop.

Fortunately the weather forecast had been accurate (for a change) and the heavy rain only lasted about fifteen minutes, so we didn't lose too much walking time, and we felt refreshed by the drinks, and carried on into Midhurst. Pete and Chris met us at the first pub we came to in Midhurst, as they had been driving along the A 272 from east to west looking for us, and we ate a very good lunch together, while Pete told us about the accommodation he had found at Coolham. It sounded ideal, although a little further from our projected halt than we would have chosen, but Chris told us not to worry, they were happy to pick us up and take us there.

After lunch, at about half past two, we set off again along the dreaded A 272, north out of Midhurst, over the River Rother, (which made us feel close to home) then turning right to head east once more along the most picturesque part of the A 272 past Cowdray Park, where the posh people hob-nob with Royals on the polo pitches! There were no alternatives to the A 272 this afternoon, so we just had to get on with it, but at least we had started to catch up on our lost mileage! Our boots were still slightly damp from the soaking they got yesterday, and Neil was once again suffering more than I was, but he wanted us to make up as much mileage as we could, so on we tramped through Halfway Bridge and Tillington, then at just before five o'clock, sooner than we had expected, we reached Petworth. This meant that we were now only about two miles short of our original stopping point for the day, and we were justifiably proud of ourselves.

We found a watering hole with a sign outside advertising "Fullers London Pride", and that was where we stopped! After a pint I thought it might be a good idea to call Chris and Pete to come and pick us up, only to discover that mobile phone reception in Petworth is almost non existent! I walked up and down the narrow streets of this small town looking for a phone box, but the only one I found was temporarily out of order, so I sent a "text message" to their phone detailing where we were, and went back for another beer! My mobile had sent the text message, but there were no guarantees that Chris and Pete would get it within the next hour, so we settled down in a corner of the pub and supped slowly at our pints, wondering when our saviours would arrive!

Eventually a head peered round the corner of the bar, and Chris turned to Pete and said "Found them!", and proceeded to the bar to order a beer. Chris returned to our table bearing four pint glasses of foaming beer, and sat down to tell us how lucky we were that they had got our message: Neither Chris nor Pete had ever received a text message before, and when their phone had bleeped telling them that my message had arrived, they sat there and looked at each other, wondering what the noise had been! Chris eventually looked at the display on the phone, and they sat there and worked out how to read the message! We sat and laughed together and drank another pint (just to be sociable you understand!) discussing the day's walk, and the pros and cons of the A 272, before levering ourselves off our seats and walking stiffly to the car for our lift to Coolham. It was a journey of about a dozen miles or so, and I think both Neil and I went to sleep for all but a mile of it! We had covered about twenty eight miles today, in some foul weather for a short time, all of it on tarmac, and our legs were aching from the constant pounding, not to mention the throbbing sensations in our boots.

We arrived at Coolham at a quarter to seven, to the "motel" we had been booked into, small chalet style rooms with even smaller shower/wash rooms behind, and drew lots for who went first in the shower! We then spent about half an hour after our showers drying and pampering our blistered feet, applying plasters where necessary, and easing them into the softest footwear we had with us for the evening. Then we went to find Pete and Chris at the pub, The Selsey Arms, 200 yards up the road.

During a very pleasant evening, we (as usual) got chatting to some of the locals, who seemed fairly indifferent to our adventure, and were less than generous when we mentioned donations. Before long we drifted off into a small side bar and after we had eaten, we got involved in a conversation with a pleasant chap in his late fifties I should imagine, who showed a great deal more interest, and who turned out to be the landlord. He invited us to breakfast in the morning and instructed the staff not to charge us, arranged for us to stay there the following night, and wrote a cheque out for £100 for our walk. Not a bad night at all!! The food had been nothing short of excellent, and although the Harveys Best was too sweet for my liking, the London Pride went down very well indeed!

It was about ten thirty when we decided to make tracks for bed, and after the short walk back to the motel, we were asleep as soon as our heads hit the pillows. We had pored over the map earlier in the evening and decided to keep to the A 272 all day tomorrow, as we had done so well today. We knew we wouldn't enjoy the walk as much, but it served the purpose to help us make good mileage, and that was the priority at the moment.

Thursday 30th May. Up at half past seven, feeling good, and ready to tackle another hard day. We walked over to the Selsey Arms for breakfast, which was almost as good as the meal we had had the night before, and then Pete and Chris took us back to Petworth, dropping us there at nine o'clock.

We made good time along the A 272, feeling all the time that the traffic was much lighter today, and we reached Wisborough Green at half past ten. Here we spent ten minutes sheltering in a bus stop while a short sharp shower passed, glad of the opportunity for a smoke, and I made a call to Roger Francis, the N.C.H. rep. who had promised to try and get some publicity on the radio or television for us. He said he was having trouble getting any interest but he would try again. He had been trying all avenues for publicity for the last three weeks, as had we, and we had had the same results all round.

We decided to get togged up with our waterproofs as the traffic would now throw all the gutter spray all over us, before setting off again for Billingshurst, another two miles down the road. As we dodged the traffic, which was beginning to build again now, close to the River Arun, I noticed a small bird flitting about in a roadside bush. I stopped Neil and we watched as a goldcrest hopped about the branches no more than six feet from us, as oblivious to the heavy traffic charging by within a few feet as it was to us, the same distance away. I had always thought that the goldcrest was a shy bird, more likely to be seen in wooded areas in the countryside, and certainly not normally seen next to a busy road, but I guess this just goes to show the adaptability of nature.

We came into Billingshurst at ten past eleven and decided to dispense with our waterproofs. Although we were aware that we may have to put them back on soon, it was a welcome respite from the sweaty horrible confines! Billingshurst seems to be one of those places that would be quite pleasant if it didn't have a major road junction slap bang in the middle of it. The A 272 and A 29 cross here, and we walked quickly through, continuing on the 272 through some quite lovely countryside through Coneyhurst arriving back in Coolham at just after twelve o'clock for a pint of lime and soda at the Selsey Arms.

The route from here on was almost dead straight, heading due east on the A 272 across the A 24 to the south of Horsham, and on to Cowfold. It would be a boring walk, but once we reached Cowfold we could divert onto minor roads heading north-east until we decided to halt for the day. We were getting quite excited now, all the place names were familiar and the road numbers were commonplace, and we realised we were getting close to Kent. Pete and Chris had said they were happy to wait for a call and pick us up from wherever we wanted, so we didn't have to plan a finish point for the day, just keep on walking until we felt the need to stop.

We trudged wearily on along the Godforsaken A 272 for another five or six miles to Cowfold, and stopped at The Coach and Horses for lunch. Our support crew must be psychic, as they met us there and had lunch with us, all the while telling us not to worry where we finished that night, they would pick us up. The encouragement they gave us that lunchtime put a bit of spring back into our step, and we set off from Cowfold at a quarter to three heading east for a mile and a bit then turning left onto a minor road signed to Warninglid. We wondered what sort of a container needed a lid with a warning? Climbing up from the A 272 into the peace and quiet of the Sussex countryside was like stepping into a foot spa after running a marathon! The silence was deafening, and the return to the countryside was a joy. Although we were climbing for the first mile or so, it was as though we had subconsciously reserved some energy for this last stretch, and the miles rolled away almost effortlessly.

At four o'clock we were in Warninglid, and we stopped to consult the map as to which way to aim next. We were only a mile and a half from our original projected overnight stopping point, so we could have stopped there, but we needed to feel that we had beaten the course, and the next psychological barrier was to cross the A 23. We headed east from Warninglid on the B 2115 and came to the A 23 at Pitts Head Crossroads where we took a minor road which led us almost directly north, just to the east of the A 23 to Staplefield, where we called a halt for the night. We were now a mile and a half past our original planned stop, and were well chuffed with ourselves. I still have trouble understanding how Neil managed to carry on after all the problems he had had with blisters, but I suppose it just means he wanted to do it just as much as I did.

We called Pete and Chris as we walked along the side of the green at Staplefield towards The Victory pub, and told them where to meet us, then turned in to the car park, and through the door into a friendly little boozer. Then I panicked! All the beer pumps I could see were Courage pumps, and I don't like Courage beers! As the sweat broke out on my brow, the landlord asked what he could do for us, and I spotted a pump on the far end of the bar, the sign on which I couldn't see. "What's on the pump at the end there, Boss?". "Oh that's just a temporary beer until we get a delivery from Courage. It's Shepherd Neame's Spitfire ale.". "Well I think we'd better try two pints of that then, thanks!". Spitfire is one of my all time favourite beers, so I guess I got very lucky that day!

It turned out that the pub was being run by a holding agency while it was being sold, and the manager had not been there long, and the barmaid who was helping him was his niece. After a while a couple of chaps approached us asking what we were doing, as they had seen us earlier in the day, as well as yesterday, on the A 272. The fact that our T-shirts proclaimed "LANDS END TO LENHAM 2002" was obviously not enough of a clue for them, and we explained our mission, and struck up a conversation with them. It was five thirty by the time Pete and Chris arrived, and we were deep in conversation by then. The barmaid had joined in and was just telling us where her accent came from, as I had just taken a bet with one of the locals that she was from East Anglia. He reckoned Dorset.

"I live in Salhouse, just between the Royal Oak and the Anglers Rest, opposite Woodfordes' brewery. The river runs along the bottom of my garden." That did it! All thoughts of the bet were gone and I gently slid to one knee and proposed! "Will you marry me?". Short silence, then an incredulous "What?!!". Well, as I explained, she must be every man's dream. A river full of fish at the end of her garden, a choice of pubs within wobbling distance, and an award winning independent brewery on the doorstep in case the pubs are shut!!! We're so shallow, us men!!

As the lady in question retreated to the relative safety of the serving area blushing furiously, my thoughts returned to the wager, and I claimed my pint! It was Woodfordes that gave it away for me: I knew the brewery was in Norfolk. My pint was duly placed on the bar, along with three more, for Neil, Chris and Pete, and the conversation resumed until Chris pointed out that it was now nearly seven o'clock and we should be heading back to the Selsey Arms. That was one of the best early evening pubs we had come across so far, and it was a shame to leave, but we also knew that the evening was going to be a good one, so after I apologised to the lovely barmaid for embarrassing her we said goodbye to the locals, and gathered our gear.

As we were leaving, one of the locals came over and whispered in my ear that he thought we were doing a marvellous job, and pressed a twenty pound note into my hand. He then told me that all our talk of the hardships of the walk, and the physical and psychological exertions which we had overcome had reminded him of the last time he had walked that sort of distance day after day: It had been in the Falklands, and he was among the soldiers who had "yomped" across the islands to liberate Port Stanley. My pain and discomfort suddenly shrivelled away as I realised that our little amble along the country lanes was so insignificant, and that this guy had not only walked in much worse conditions than we had encountered, he had also carried a 100 lb pack on his back, and a firearm of some description. And he had an irate Sergeant-Major screaming at him most of the way! I take my hat off to him.

Pete drove us back to the Selsey Arms, where we were shown to our beautiful chalet style rooms, had a quick shower, got changed and met Pete and Chris in the bar. During the day I had spoken to one of my old mates, Wilf, who lives in Worthing, and he was going to meet us in the pub later in the evening, so we got the eating out of the way, and when Wilf arrived with his girlfriend Sarah, we had a good old chinwag and a few beers. Neil was hitting the London Pride with a vengeance, and I suppose I was doing fairly well, and as Wilf, Sarah and I sat in a recessed compartment chatting with Pete and Chris, I looked round to see Neil gazing deep into the eyes of a lovely young waitress, who was letting him know in no uncertain terms what a magnificent effort she thought he was making on this walk. I started making arrangements to stay the night at Wilf's place, as I had no desire to share a twin room with a pair of starry eyed lovebirds, and Chris agreed to come to Worthing in the morning to collect me. So that was settled! Then, all of a sudden, Neil was on his own again, so we cancelled the sleeping arrangements and carried on as we were. Neil offered no explanation, so I asked no questions, and we got another beer and carried on chatting away to each other.

It had been a very good evening, but, as all good things, it had to come to an end, and we said goodnight to Wilf and Sarah, and headed for bed. We needed a good night's rest, and after the beer we had consumed, I would have been very surprised if either of us didn't sleep well!

Friday 31st May. The Selsey Arms is situated on the junction of the A 272 and the B 2139, which is quite a busy junction, and we awoke at seven forty five to the muffled sound of heavy traffic grinding its way across the crossroads. As we were performing our ablutions Neil suddenly asked me if I had noticed the girl he had been talking to the previous night in the bar. When I said that I had, he asked me what had happened to her!! He had been so drunk that he hadn't even got her name, offered her a drink, or anything, and when I told him how she had been looking at him, he looked like a gambler who had thrown away a winning hand!! He was inconsolable as we made our way across the lawn to the pub for breakfast, and his hopes of her being there to serve breakfast were dashed when we saw the landlord rushing around with plates of steaming bacon, eggs, sausages, mushrooms, baked beans, tomatoes and toast. Mind you, after we had munched our way through that lot there was no look of woe on his face, just a look of indigestion and wind!

Pete and Chris took us back to Staplefield, and dropped us at nine o'clock where we had finished the previous day, and as this was their last day looking after us, we said goodbye to them. Off they went to drop our gear at Rusthall, where I had arranged to stay with friends for the night, and we set off in brilliant sunshine and with the promise of good weather for the rest of the day.

Our planned route took us across mid-Sussex heading almost directly east as far as Ardingly, and the vast majority of the morning was to be on footpaths. As the weather had been quite good yesterday, and was superb this morning, we didn't envisage any major problems, and were laughing and joking as we set off onto the first of the footpaths. We made our way through Tyes Place, and followed the well maintained footpath right to the edge of the flood. There we stopped, had a long look at the map to try and find an alternative footpath route, had a quick scout around to see if we could skirt around the huge expanse of water, then gave up, turned round and retraced our steps to the road at Tyes Place! The alternatives looked pretty rough going, and we had no guarantees that they would be any drier in the low lying areas than the path we had just tried. So we did our usual, and went by road!

A very minor road, little more than a track really, took us directly north through some stunning countryside for a couple of miles to a junction about two miles north-east of Handcross, where we turned right along Handcross Lane towards Balcombe. On arrival at Balcombe we took a tiny lane once again, just to the north of the village, heading due east dropping steeply into a lovely valley before it crossed the north-western arm of the Ardingly Reservoir. As we climbed the other side of the valley, Neil was attending the call of nature behind a hedge and I was poring over the map when I heard a car approaching, and not wanting to get run over now we had made it this far, I jumped up the steep verge to allow easy passage to said vehicle. I need not have bothered. It was Pete and Chris, and as they pulled up next to us Chris said "What are you doing out here?" I replied that we had had to alter course due to the flooded footpaths, and then asked him what they were doing here, as we had expected them to go straight home. "We're lost!" was the grinning answer! So we directed them to Forest Row and told them we'd meet them there for lunch, before continuing on our way across the peninsula to drop just as steeply to the north-eastern arm of the reservoir, across a viaduct, then up again to Ardingly village. (This route was just confirmation to Neil that I was the "Hill Magician"! He has told several people since the walk that if they are ever in need of a hill, he knows the man to provide it!). It was now eleven o'clock, and we were behind time, so we grabbed a carton of fruit juice each from a corner shop, and carried on, now heading almost north again to West Hoathly, where we turned right to head due east again, aiming to reach Forest Row for lunch. We had to keep up a good pace as we had added about five miles to our route because of the flood, which was difficult as the terrain was far from flat, but we made fairly good time, walking through some pretty heathland and lovely quiet wooded areas on the north edge of the Ashdown Forest, the traffic being the only bugbear.

Just after we had crossed the Greenwich Meridian, a couple of miles south of the Weir Wood Reservoir, we turned left, heading north-east towards Forest Row. Then we were surprised by the tooting of a car horn, and as we looked at each other and commented that we could have done with that all the way from Lands End, Pete and Chris pulled up next to us again! "Wanna lift mate?" said Chris! When we politely declined his kind offer (I think the word "off" came into it somewhere!) he said "Well bloody hurry up then, we're starving!" We stopped for lunch at one fifteen in a pub on the B 2110 in Forest Row, and I glanced at the television while we were there and saw that Senegal were beating France in the first game of the 2002 World Cup!!! That'll do for me!

A very filling tuna baguette and chips later, we said our goodbyes again to Pete and Chris, and thanked them again for their support, and set off to the east along the B 2110 for about a mile before joining the Forest Way, which would lead us all the way to Groombridge and the Kent border. It was six or seven miles to Groombridge, and all of it flat, as the path is laid on a disused railway line which follows the valley of the River Medway until about a mile short of Groombridge. This was a welcome respite from the hills of the morning, and we made excellent time along here. Neil timed us along one section and we covered three miles in forty one minutes. That equates to nearly four and a half miles an hour!

We passed just to the north of Hartfield on the Forest Way, and shortly afterwards we decided to take a short detour to the north of the River Medway. Over a footbridge and up to the stile the other side, and we were in paradise! The sun had been shining all day, and we revelled in it, and this beautiful setting on a sunny spring afternoon was really special. We dawdled along this path, idling the whole two miles of it, listening with bated breath to the symphony of birdsong which accompanied us, justifying our sudden bout of laziness by referring back to the hardships of the last fortnight, and ensuring that we didn't strain so much as a bootlace! The daisies shook their heads in laughter with us, and the trees stood as if in a guard of honour, clapping their leaves occasionally to welcome us back to our home county.

The path rejoined the disused railway track a mile short of Groombridge, and we made our way up into the village happy in the knowledge that another four miles would see us at Rosie and Gregs' house for a restful evening. When we crossed the County Boundary into Kent, just between the village and Groombridge Place, we made a decision that we really ought to celebrate this landmark with a pint, so we headed for The Crown, a pub I know from my Morris dancing days. The pub sits just to the north of the entrance to Groombridge Place, and we had to pass right by it, so it would have been rude not to stop there, wouldn't it! As it was we had to pass it by, as the landlord must have detected our approach and bolted the doors! Sod you then, we'll take our custom elsewhere!

Although we could have murdered a beer there, we carried on, following the road now, up Groombridge Hill to join the A 264 just west of Langton Green. The next pub we came across was The Hare, which sits on a corner of the green, and offered a welcoming pint of Greene King ale. We reached the Hare at about ten past six, which meant we had walked for eight hours. During the day we had covered almost exactly thirty miles, which worked out at an average of three and three quarter miles per hour.

I phoned Rosie to let her know where we were as we ordered our second pints, and then phoned a taxi to take us from the pub to Rosie and Gregs' place as it was about a mile off our route. Timing was perfect, as the taxi turned up just as we finished our beers, and we threw our packs and bits and bobs into the boot and climbed in. Five minutes later we were in Rusthall and saying hello to the Holder family, Rosie, a friend of mine from years ago, Greg, her husband, and Theo and James, their sons. Greg showed us to our room, and we had a quick shower and got changed then went downstairs to present our human side! Steph, Rosie's sister, another good friend of mine had arrived, and we gratefully accepted a couple of beers from Greg while we decided what to have to eat.

Greg and I left the others to acquaint themselves and walked a couple of hundred yards up the road to get an Indian takeaway, having a good old chinwag on the way. We had known each other for about sixteen years, but this was only the second time we had met in the last fifteen, and we still get on like we used to. Arriving back at Greg's laden with various curries and accompaniments we were swiftly relieved of our load and told to sort the drinks out while the girls dished up, which suited us fine! I chose to stick with the beer, as I didn't fancy a raging hangover in the morning, and wine always does that to me, but Neil decided to risk a glass of white, and we sat down to dinner in a house other than a public house for the first time in three weeks!

We enjoyed a wonderfully convivial evening in some of the best company I could wish for, and didn't visit the pub all night! Chatting about old times and the changes we've all gone through, I realised that this walk was the biggest achievement of my life, and Neil says the same goes for him. I think everybody should do something like this at some point in their lives: It really gives you a sense of purpose. Sneaking outside for a cigarette every now and then made me feel like a schoolboy again, chatting to Rosie and Steph brought back my late teens and early twenties, talking to Greg reminded me of my mid to late twenties, and Neil was there to remind me that I was now the wrong side of forty!!!

We went to bed at about midnight knowing that we were nearly home: A day and a half more on the road and we would be back in Lenham. What was that going to feel like?! I think we were still discussing our feelings when Neil began to snore. Or was it me snoring? Who cares?!!

Chapter 8

The Home Straight

Tunbridge Wells to Lenham

Saturday 1st June. We woke at a quarter to seven on this beautiful Saturday morning, the sun already warming the spring air, and the dew rising in little clouds of vapour off the grass of Rosie and Gregs' garden.. Having washed and dressed I made my way downstairs to be greeted by Rosie calling to me that our support crew had turned up. It was only half past seven, and Neil was still washing, so they would have to wait a while, but I went back upstairs and packed my stuff and brought it down to get it out of the way. Mike, half of our support crew was stood in the doorway looking as though he had just woken from a terrible nightmare. Either that or he was horribly hungover! Bruce, the other half of the support crew was sitting in the car looking impatient, so we told Neil to take his time, and had a cup of tea while he packed his gear away. I had arranged for Bruce to collect our belongings at eight thirty, so it was his own fault for turning up an hour early!

We got rid of Bruce and Mike at seven forty five and had a small breakfast of cereal and more tea before setting off towards Tunbridge Wells, the good wishes of our hosts ringing in our ears. We made our way out of Rusthall, up over the common and onto the A 264, turning left to follow the road along the top of Tunbridge Wells common, past the Spa and the Royal Wells hotels. The main road was already busy and we were glad of the pavement all the way. We reached the town centre at just before nine o'clock and decided that we had not filled our bellies enough at Rusthall (our own fault, not our hosts, I hasten to add), so we went into Royal Victoria Place and ordered a coffee, a bacon roll and a sausage roll each from a cafe-type place and sat there in our boots, combat trousers, T-shirts handwritten with "LANDS END TO LENHAM 2002" and "THE LUNATICS LURCH 2002" while all the early morning shoppers looked at us disdainfully and wondered what we were doing sullying their pristine shopping centre with our presence.

We left the Royal Victoria Place by the back entrance (so as not to offend anyone further!!!) and found our way back to the A 264 and followed that to Pembury. Barb phoned me to ask where we were staying overnight, and when I said we hadn't organised anywhere, she took charge and said she would sort something out, but Bruce and Mike wouldn't be able to deliver our stuff, so we'd have to sort that out ourselves. No problem, I phoned Mouse, who had said when he left us that if we needed anything just call and consider it done, and left a message on his voicemail asking him to contact me about picking up our gear and delivering it to the Headcorn area once we had some digs organised.

When we reached Pembury we crossed the bypass and turned right into the old village, thereby avoiding the majority of the traffic, and came out on the bypass about a mile from the Kippings Cross roundabout. We tried to find a path to keep us off the dual carriageway, and thought we had cracked it when we found the remains of the old road, but this only lasted about a hundred yards before rejoining the main A 21! We walked along the verge of the main road, then at the roundabout we turned left onto the Matfield road, where we fought the traffic for the entire three miles into Matfield. There are no footpaths along this piece of road, and the traffic treats it like a racetrack. We had decided that although the weather was good, we would stick to roads today rather than going and buying a map: We both knew our way by roads, and I had forgotten all about a map for the area that we already knew, so we were slightly stuffed as far as footpaths were concerned! Never mind, we were buzzing with the thought of being nearly home, and stopping to look at the scenery was at the bottom of the list of priorities today. Shame really, because as I mentioned at the beginning of the book, we take so little notice of the beautiful countryside that we all know so well, we take it for granted.

As we walked into Matfield we spotted a small tea room in the old post office, and thought it was time for some refreshment, so in we went to be greeted by a lovely young thing who asked us what we would like. I became very nervous until Neil pulled himself together and asked for a pot of tea for two and some sticky cakes. The look in his eye said he would like a lot more than that!! The tea rooms are very traditional, and kept in the fashion of the 1950s, with bone china crockery and delicate little tea spoons and pastry forks hardly suitable for two hairy lunatics who would have quite happily drunk their tea out of a bucket at this moment! The tables and chairs were all either antique or very good reproduction, the floor was bare boards, and the walls were part panelled, part plaster, and decorated with posters from the past such as the old Colmans Mustard or Bovril or Players Navy Cut placards that you find in junk/antique shops. It was a smashing little time warp, and with a wonderful welcome, and I would recommend it to anyone!

After our little sojourn we carried on up to the north end of the village where we turned right onto the Brenchley road, once again dodging the traffic, although it wasn't so frequent on this road, until we reached Brenchley village where we went left following the smaller lanes now towards Marden. Passing a house with a sign outside informing us that its name was "Little Miners", Neil patted the imaginary head of a three foot tall Scargillite, chuckling to himself. "Minor Miners" he said, to which I replied "Mine are Minor Miners too"! This kept our warped senses of humour happy for another half a mile or so, the occasional chuckle escaping our otherwise silent lips. It was comparatively peaceful along the lanes, and we slowed our pace a bit to enjoy the smell of the countryside and the sounds that can only be heard miles from town. Peace of mind was the order of the day when Barb phoned to say she had found us a B.& B. in Headcorn, and we uttered the name "Headcorn" with some reverence a few times, as if we couldn't believe we'd made it this far! The sun was hot again and I was beginning to rue the fact that I had worn a sleeveless T-shirt, as the tops of my arms were now bright pink!

We were now on roads which I knew quite well, and we headed for the White Hart at Claygate (remember Wimborne and Martin Cleggett the archaeologist?) for lunch. During a pleasant lunch the Aussie barmaid was questioning us about our T-shirts and asked where Lenham was. This was the first time we had been asked this question, and we found it ironic that we should be so close to home before having to answer it! All the way from Lands End we had met people who knew where we were going, and fifteen miles from home we meet an Antipodean who, having been in Kent for two months, has never visited the best village in the world! A fine pint of lime and soda helped wash our lunch down, and we were on our way once more.

Cutting through the lanes to the south of Marden, the sun still beating down and very little shade to be had, we slowed considerably, and had frequent water/cigarette breaks. We had crossed the main Horsmonden to Marden road and were heading for Staplehurst when our afternoon's entertainment came cycling towards us. Head down and pedalling furiously, a lycra-clad streak of finely honed muscle on a bike shot by and screeched to a halt ten yards past us, and the rider asked in a squeaky nasal voice "Are you on a sponsored walk?". Stifling our chuckles at the strange voice and the stupid question, we turned to face the inquisitor, and Neil answered in the affirmative. "Oh, I thought so as soon as I saw you, but I haven't heard anything on the radio about a sponsored walk, so I didn't know. Where have you come from?"! We politely pointed out the slogans on our T-shirts, then had to explain that we hadn't walked all that distance today, and had started the day just the other side of Tunbridge Wells.

The guy must have thought that we were trying to prove to him that we were super fit or something, and started to tell us about himself: "I applied to join the Army when I was younger, but they said I was too fit. I know you have to be fit in the Army, and I cycle about thirty miles every day with a little bit of shopping in my rucksack." indicating with his thumb the small knapsack on his back. "I must be fitter than most soldiers, because they don't do that every day, do they?!". Neil almost choked himself attempting to stifle a giggle, and I couldn't keep a straight face as we silently nodded our agreement. "I'm surprised I haven't heard about this walk, because I do a lot for "Talk-Sport" radio on Saturday nights, and there hasn't been anything on there about it." he said, and I admitted that they were one of the few radio stations I hadn't contacted for publicity. "Well, there you go, see! I could have sung you a song, 'coz that's what I do, and we could've let people know.". I then had a brainwave! "If we give you some details could you do a bit for us tonight? We are stopping in Headcorn tonight, and could do with some publicity for the last few miles of the walk tomorrow morning.". "No, I don't do Saturday nights! Phew, it's warm today, isn't it?!" he said, unzipping the tight lycra top he was wearing to reveal a knitted woollen "tank-top"! No wonder he was hot! We exchanged a few more pleasantries with him and made our confused and amazed way towards Staplehurst. After a mile or so of almost silent walking, punctuated now and then by a snigger, we simultaneously collapsed in hysterics. Neil was on his knees in the road, and I was fortunate enough to find a fence to hold me up, but we were both incapable of walking for a couple of minutes! We laughed so much we couldn't breathe properly, and it took a good five minutes for us to regain our composure enough to carry on! Neil says that the guy was sent by God as a reward for getting that far through all the pain and mental stress!!

We carried on into Staplehurst and crossed the main A 229 Hastings road at the traffic lights, glad of a bit of verge to ease the pounding of boots on tarmac, and decided to stop for the day when we reached The Hawkenbury pub. As we walked these last couple of miles, crossing the beautiful River Buelt, I continually tried to phone Mouse to arrange transportation of our gear from The Red Lion to Headcorn, where our B. & B. had been arranged, but it seemed that his phone must be switched off. We arrived at The Hawkenbury and got ourselves a pint each before I called Mouse one last time and left a message on his answerphone to call me within the next ten minutes or we'd make other arrangements. Fifteen minutes later I phoned Drew, who I knew was staying (with Alison!) at Mum's in Lenham, and he agreed to bring our stuff down. A pint later Alison and Drew arrived and took us to our final guest house of the walk!

We arrived at the guest house at about half past six and arranged to meet Alison and Drew later that evening in the George and Dragon before lugging our packs up to the front door. The landlady answered the door and the look of horror on her face told us that we were not a pretty sight! After a quick chat she seemed to take pity on us and ushered us in and showed us to our room, ensuring that we knew it was a non smoking house, and pointing out the shower room! We spent the first half hour flat on our backs on our lovely soft beds (having taken our boots off first!), trying to find the energy to walk to the shower room, and recalling the events of the day. When Neil said "Just think, three weeks ago we were in Truro!", I realised that I had forgotten more about the walk than I thought, and I had to pick up the diary and remind us both of some of the events of the past three weeks! We swore about the weather, laughed at the jokes and silly situations, and generally mused over the various scenarios we had found ourselves in, when my mobile phone rang. It was Mouse asking where to deliver our gear!! He explained that he had got my message that morning then went out for a ride on his Harley, and turned his phone off! We were not impressed, but never mind, we were all sorted now so forget it!

By the time we had showered and changed into some relatively decent clothes it was a quarter past eight, and we were ready for some more beer and some food, so we made our way downstairs and asked the landlady for a key "as we may be late in". She was entertaining a young female (note I didn't say "lady") in the kitchen, and they seemed to be sniggering at something, and we got the impression that we were interrupting something. From the reaction to our request you would have thought we had asked to take the telly with us! She couldn't work out why we wanted to stay out late, and it took us a good five minutes to persuade her that we would look after her precious key and bring it back safe and sound, before she reluctantly handed it over! We exited the guest house and turned left towards the pub. "I don't reckon we'd have much luck with those two!" said Neil, and I collapsed laughing! As if we would be interested in a pair of "velvet tippers"!!

As soon as we got to the George and Dragon we ordered some food, (I think it was Lasagne, but I couldn't swear to it!) and the regulation two pints of bitter, hoping that we could finish our solids before Alison and Drew turned up. No such luck, they arrived just as the food did, so they had to watch us eat for a few minutes before the conversation really got going. After we had eaten, we decided to move on, as the beer was not really to our liking, so Alison drove us to the Smarden Bell, where we knew we would have a good selection of beers and a good atmosphere. The conversation was all a bit one sided, with Alison and Drew asking questions about various aspects of the walk, and Neil and I relating the best bits along with some of the low points. The evening went by all too quickly and Alison and Drew left at ten o'clockish and I booked us a taxi for eleven fifteen so we had time for another couple of pints (as if we needed them!). I don't recall too much of that evening, the euphoria had taken over, and no, that isn't the name of a beer!. All I know is that we woke up at the B. & B., so I assume the taxi must have turned up!! And I must also assume that we slept well!!!

Sunday 2nd June. We were woken at seven thirty by the sunlight sneaking through a gap in the curtains, and we lay there chatting about anything and nothing for a while before summoning the energy to get up! We didn't mention the few miles that we had left to cover to complete our adventure, I think because we were feeling sad that it was nearly over. We washed, dressed, and went downstairs for breakfast at about eight o'clock, to be greeted by the landlady who seemed to have stolen all our enthusiasm, and was bright and bubbly this morning. Neil was the first to ask the question which had been in both our minds for the last day or two: "What's it going to feel like when we get to Lenham?". Our thoughts were mixed, muddled, however you like to describe them, and we knew that we could not predict how we would feel.

Mike arrived at nine, and we loaded the car for the last time and headed for Hawkenbury where yesterday's walk had terminated. After Mike left us Neil started to worry that we would not make the distance by half past twelve, and as this was the prearranged time for our arrival in Lenham we started marching at a fair pace. It was nine twenty five when we commenced our final day, and for timing's sake we divided it into three stages: Three miles to Headcorn, three and a half from Headcorn to Grafty Green, and three and a half from Grafty Green to Lenham. This meant we could keep an eye accurately on our timing. We reached the crossroads in Headcorn at ten past ten, and carried straight on towards Grafty, sweating under the baking sun, and grateful of the breeze as and when it wafted over us.

We had been led to believe that some people from Lenham were going to meet us somewhere along the way and walk back into Lenham with us, and we resolved to stay shoulder to shoulder all the way, no matter who wanted to get between us! Other than this brief conversation we were almost silent all the way to the King's Head at Grafty, where Ken, the landlord supplied two pints of lime and soda, pleased to have the extra bodies in there by the look of things! It was now a quarter past eleven and the first World Cup game involving England was on the television, and if Ken had been expecting a crowd he was sorely disappointed. There were no more than a dozen people in there, so I took the opportunity to watch ten minutes of the match and shout a few encouraging comments, and Neil dragged me away at twenty five past, insisting that we should make a move now, as there was still a big hill to climb! I had forgotten about that!

We decided on Boughton Hill as opposed to Liverton, as the road would be quieter and it was a prettier route, but I suppose with everyone watching England's heroics on the football pitch, it would have been as quiet either way. We climbed the hill to Boughton Church and stopped outside to admire the view. It's a scene that has always been special to me, the view is spectacular and goes on for ever it seems, looking out over the Weald of Kent, south-west to well beyond Cranbrook, and south-east to Tenterden and beyond. On a clear day, I have been told you can see the ridge of hills just to the north of Hastings! The view is 180 degrees of proper Kent countryside, and it always seems so tranquil. I love it.

. After five minutes we set off again up over the crest of the hill, and on over the Boughton crossroads where the chalk cross on the North Downs above Lenham came into view. This was the moment I had been working towards, and the lump in my throat would have stopped any conversation, had there been any going on! That landmark has marked my return to Lenham every time I have come back to the village, and I'm talking about from when I was a kid and had been out fishing or for a bike ride. Thirty five years I've been admiring that view! We almost floated down the gradual slope of the Boughton Road to the entrance of Chilston Park, from where I phoned the pub to tell them that we were nearly there, and was told that we must slow down, they weren't ready yet!! We had a cigarette break and took a slow wander up to the crossroads by the White Horse, where Neil suggested that we go in and get pissed, as we had not specified where in Lenham we were going to finish!!!

Once we had laughed this idea off we ambled slowly up past Oxley House and along to the main Headcorn road, turning right, noting that this was the last junction we would negotiate before turning left through the door of the Red Lion! Still nobody had met us to walk alongside us, and we began to feel as if everyone had forgotten we were coming home today. Where were the television crews and the radio men with their huge furry microphones? Never mind, as we walked round the corner by Inkstand Farm, Alison and Drew and my Mum were walking towards us. Greetings were warm and heartfelt, and I felt sorry that none of

Neil's family had come to meet him, although my family were making almost as much fuss of him as they were of me!

We still didn't feel any real emotion; a bit of a buzz maybe, but nothing spectacular, and we posed for Drew to take some photos of us shaking hands over the Lenham village sign, before wandering slowly over the railway bridge and down the High Street. A few people came out of their houses as we walked by, but I think this was by chance. I suppose we had been expecting more of a welcome home than this, but we weren't too bothered: All we wanted was to get to the pub and do some serious refreshing!

Gez and Neil
Congratulating each other on their respective dress sense and hairstyle!!
Or on reaching their goal

As we walked round the corner by the Working Mens' Club, our view of the Square was obstructed by about a hundred people crowding the junction and cheering! John Barrett was outside his house doing some maintenance and came over to shake our hands, and the cat-calls from the Square floated up the High Street to us "Come on! Your beer's getting warm!", and "Hurry up, I haven't got all day to stand here cheering!". (Apparently the crowd in the Square had held up a wedding car on its way to the Church, telling the Bride that our return to the village was more important than her wedding! If you're the Bride who got married on 2nd June 2002 and got held up by a baying mob in Lenham Square, please accept my apology!). So we made our way the last hundred yards to the Square.

I still couldn't tell you what I felt as we entered the village proper. My emotions were all mixed up, and when Barb appeared in front of us with a tray containing two foaming jugs of beer, I handed mine to somebody, anybody, and hugged her for what seemed like several minutes. Then I had to prise Neil away from some young lady and shake his hand. As we looked into each other's eyes the emotions came to the top, and we hugged each other, laughing and repeating over and over "We've done it!". Then we grabbed our beers and went into the pub.

The celebrations were still going on a few hours later, and I needed to get showered and changed, so I offered Neil the use of our bathing facilities and a change of clothes, but he wanted to get home and relax under his own roof, understandably. Barb and I wandered up the road and I had a lazy bath before changing into clean, dry, ironed clothes, and returning to the pub to meet Neil.

The evening passed uneventfully and both Neil and I were grateful for that. We had had enough excitement over the last three weeks, and it was nice to return to normality! Whatever that was!!

Gez (on the left of the picture) and Neil wearing big smiles (and boots!) as they walk the last few yards into the village

A well earned pint, the first of many to be consumed that day!

Opposite: A section of the crowd awaiting our arrival in Lenham Square

Epilogue

After all the celebrations had finished, and our feet had started to recover, the true enormity of what we had done started to hit home. Neither of us had ever taken on a challenge like this before, and although we had struggled both mentally and physically at certain points along the way, we had never seriously considered giving up. We had not thought of it as a huge challenge either!

Every now and then when somebody else came up to me and put their arm round my shoulder to congratulate me on my achievement, I would feel a bit more proud, and I think it will be a long time before it actually hits home that we walked almost the entire width of the country at its widest point! This "arm round the shoulder" stuff happened quite frequently for about a month, and although I appreciated the gesture and the good wishes that came my way, I think they would have been more welcome had they been shared with Neil. He got to the stage of greeting me in the pub on a Friday evening and saying "You did ever so well on that walk!". I do wish that people had recognised his achievement as well as mine!!

The most frequently asked question since we got back to Lenham has been "Would you do it again?". Neil and I both agree that this question cannot be answered! We had such an amazingly good time while we were walking, that you would think the answer would be an instantaneous "Yes", but we also know that you can never recreate the atmosphere of an event like this, so the answer would have to be "No". We really want to do something along the same lines, but I need to recover my financial status first! I spent so much during those three weeks, added to the fact that I was not earning either, it'll take a long time to get back on an even keel!

There have been several chats about what we're going to do next, and we've talked about walking from the Scots border above Berwick-on-Tweed back to Lenham, but neither of us are getting any younger, and whether we'll ever get round to doing it I couldn't say.

Both Neil and I missed the daily routine when we had finished, and it was a real bind to have to go back to work, and our promises of continuing walking have come to nought. I walk the dog for a few miles at a time as often as I can, but it's not the same!

At the end of the cricket season I began to notice a sharp pain in my left heel, and I went to the doctor after a couple of months to be told that I have "Plantar Fasciitis", an inflammation of the support structure from the Achilles tendon to the arch of the foot. I have taken pills and potions (which I don't like doing for long periods), and I have tried resting the foot, all to no avail, so now I'm trying some gentle stretching exercises to (hopefully) regain fitness and get back into some form of training so that when we do decide to take up another challenge, I will be semi-prepared for it!

Neil does a very physical job, and this has meant that his fitness level has not really altered since before the walk. However, only about 3 months before starting the walk, he fell about 12 feet from a scaffold whilst carrying a heavy piece of timber, landing on his back, with the piece of wood on top of him and only escaped serious injury through good fortune and the fact that he was so fit in the first place. We were worried for a while that he may not have been able to start the walk, let alone finish it!

I must take this opportunity to thank everybody who helped us to complete the walk. The list is probably not all-embracing, because so many people and organisations were involved, but special thanks must go to the following: Alison and Drew Marsh, my sister and brother-in-law, our support crew for the first four days, and Drew's aunt Doreen, for putting them up (or should that read "putting up with them"?): Lyn and Phil Hollier for their support over the next four days from Fowey to Exmouth: John Barratt and his wife Michelle and their family for interrupting their holiday to help us for the four days from Exmouth to Wimborne Minster: Peter and Jean Adams, my Uncle and Aunt, for their assistance and wonderful hospitality between Wimborne and Winchester: Pete and Christian Wise for keeping us going and looking after us from Winchester to Rusthall (probably psychologically the hardest part of the walk!): and finally (in this section at least) Mike Portt and Bruce Tippen for their little bit at the end!!

Thanks for accommodation provided by Nick, of N.C.H. (The Methodist Church at Par), and his friends at Crafthole the following night; Ben Forth and his mate Bill, the finest Buffalo spirits in the West, at Newton Abbot; Uncle Peter and Auntie Jean in The New Forest; Alan Kinge, Town Crier of Winchester and his wife; Greg and Rosie Holder and family for putting us up, feeding us curry, beer, wine and then breakfast!

Thanks must go to all the guesthouses and B. & B.s we stopped at on the way who offered us discounts on their usual rates. These include the marvellous Mowhay guesthouse at Truro, The Sunningdale at Goldsithney, The Oasis at Falmouth, The Exmouth Town Council (or is it a City?) who subsidised (quite heavily!) our stay at The Beacon Hotel, The Anchor Inn at Beer, Zoar House at Puddletown, and both Righton Lodge and Stakley Lodge in Wimborne. The Landlord of the Selsey Arms in Coolham, Sussex, made a donation to the walk which was equivalent to our rooms for a night! If I have missed anyone out of this list I apologise, but you should have let us know!!!

All those who sponsored us, including Ulrich, who as I mentioned in chapter one, came up with a huge donation (worth over £1,000 in total!!) over a year after the end of the walk. The total amount raised was in excess of £4,500, and that, coupled with the fun we had in the three weeks it took us to walk the four hundred and twenty odd miles, makes it absolutely unforgettable!

Last (but by no means least) on my list of thanks is my wife, Barb. She put up with all my moaning, my all day training walks (when I really should have been working on the house!), and the financial hardships brought about by taking three and a half weeks off work to go on this glorified pub crawl, and she still kept encouraging me and helping arrange accommodation etc.. Thank you Love, I couldn't have done it without you.

Hopefully I will get this book into print late in 2003, before we decide what, if anything, we will do next. Then, if it is perused by the Directors any of the local companies who refused, forgot or otherwise failed to sponsor us, perhaps they would like to make amends the next time anybody undertakes such a task for the community! I should point out here that the "companies" I refer to are NOT the shops and small businesses around The Square, but the more major local employers.

The winding down is done now, and the walk is not much more than a distant, albeit marvellous memory. I hope that you have enjoyed this book, the laughs were by far the greatest part for us, and if it inspires one individual to commit themselves to a similar adventure in the future, then I will be happy.

Printed in the United Kingdom
by Lightning Source UK Ltd.
98611UKS00001B/23-118